Writing from Within Intro

Curtis Kelly & Arlen Gargagliano

CAMBRIDGE UNIVERSITY PRESS
Cambridge, New York, Melbourne, Madrid, Cape Town, Singapore, São Paulo, Delhi

Cambridge University Press
32 Avenue of the Americas, New York, NY 10013–2473, USA

www.cambridge.org
Information on this title: www.cambridge.org/9780521606264

Telephone numbers, e-mail addresses, and street addresses
given in this book have been created for practice purposes
only and all reasonable care has been taken to avoid using
numbers or addresses that are currently in use. However,
the publisher takes no responsibility for the inadvertent use
of actual numbers or addresses.

First published 2001
4th printing 2007

Printed in Hong Kong, China, by Golden Cup Printing Company Limited

A catalog record for this publication is available from the British Library

ISBN 978-0-521-60626-4 student's book
ISBN 978-0-521-60625-7 teacher's manual

Illustrations: Cover: Jose Ortega/Images.com; Kathryn Adams: 12, 13, 23, 30, 43, 61, 68, 71, 78, 82, 89, 94, 104, 106, 112, 118; Sheryl Dickert: 14, 19, 22, 24, 46, 48, 53, 60, 64, 72, 79, 80, 109, 113; Lynn Fellman: 15, 16, 17, 29, 41, 44, 45, 50, 54, 56, 101, 102, 110; Colleen O'Hara: 8, 10, 25, 27, 28, 36, 37, 40, 63, 81, 86, 90, 92, 93, 115, 116; William Waitzman: 4, 6, 20, 26, 33, 34, 35, 39, 42, 58, 65, 67, 74, 77, 83, 87, 91, 100, 111

Art direction, book design, and layout services: Adventure House, NYC

Contents

Plan of the book

Unit	Title	Prewriting
1	Who am I?	☐ letters of introduction ☐ topics
2	Special places	☐ setting the scene ☐ ending a personal story
3	An ideal partner	☐ putting information in order ☐ giving reasons I
4	Snapshot	☐ general information ☐ concluding sentences
5	My seal	☐ topic sentences
6	It's a party!	☐ plans and instructions ☐ planning a paragraph
7	Thank-you letter	☐ giving reasons II ☐ time markers
8	Movie review	☐ movie summaries ☐ writing more than one paragraph
9	Friendship	☐ supporting sentences
10	Superhero powers	☐ expressing wishes I
11	Advertisements	☐ claims and recommendations ☐ attention getters
12	Lessons learned	☐ giving explanations ☐ conclusions

Writing	Editing	Option
writing a letter of introduction	connecting sentences	writing addresses and signatures
writing about a special place	prepositional phrases	making a tourist guidebook
writing about an ideal partner	parallel structure	creating dating game characters
writing about a favorite photo	present or past?	making a picture time line
writing about a personal seal	commas with *because*	making a group flag
writing a notice and paragraph for a class party	*so that* and *to*	designing a party poster
writing a thank-you letter	*before* and *after*	writing a letter to a company
writing a movie review	pronouns	producing a movie
writing about a friend	combining sentences with *so*	writing a magazine article
writing about a superhero power	expressing wishes II	writing a comic book story
writing an advertisement	persuasive language	advertising for a class flea market
writing about something you regret	word choice	designing a card

To the teacher

For a student who has never written more than a single sentence at a time, drafting a whole paragraph, even a short one, is a daunting challenge. Yet by writing even short texts, a whole new avenue for communication opens up. There are things students will write that they would never say, and writing offers them the potential to go deeply into their inner worlds. We, as authors, believe that all language learners, even low-level learners, possess a need to express themselves and share what is meaningful to them.

This book was written for such learners. Our goal was to create activities that not only allow them to succeed at writing English, but also allow them to express personal, meaningful, and sometimes fanciful facets of their lives. Low-level learners, too, have inner worlds. In addition, we have tried to create activities that pull our learners into writing rather than push them.

Writing from Within Intro covers a spectrum of educational objectives. Students are taught how to write sentences, generate and organize content, structure and sequence this content into paragraphs, review and edit what they have written, and finally, how to respond to what others have written. We see writing as a balanced combination of language, expository, and self-revelation skills.

Like its predecessor, *Writing from Within*, the focus of each unit is a writing assignment. Some assignments are introspective: For example, learners are asked to reflect on something they are thankful for. Others are more conventional but task-based: Learners are asked to write movie reviews and advertisements. In this way, humanistic writing assignments are balanced with task-based writing assignments to provide a broad range of writing experiences. In addition, each unit ends with an optional expansion activity that gives learners the opportunity to apply their new skills to a different task.

At the center of each unit is a writing assignment. Five of the lessons in each unit are prewriting activities that should be completed before the first draft is written. Prewriting activities include generating and organizing information, and learning basic language structures. Expository skills, such as how to write topic and supporting sentences, are also taught. Two lessons follow the writing assignment: The editing lesson teaches learners to enrich their writing by making stylistic choices. The feedback lesson gives learners the opportunity to respond to their classmates' writing. Each unit takes 3–5 hours of class time to complete, and although the syllabus is developmental, it is not necessary to do each unit in order.

This chart shows the unit structure:

Prewriting	Brainstorming	The topic is introduced and writing ideas are generated.
	Analyzing sentences	Students analyze model sentences in the context of a paragraph.
	Prewriting and Learning about organization activities	Students generate content for their paragraphs, learn expository organizational skills, and learn how to organize their paragraphs.

Writing	Model and assignment	*Students analyze model paragraphs and receive instructions for writing their paragraphs.*
Postwriting	Editing	*Students take a closer look at language and structures and edit their writing.*
	Giving feedback	*Students exchange paragraphs with other students for review and feedback.*
	Option	*Almost a separate unit in itself, the optional writing activity helps students transfer their newly gained skills to another communicative writing task.*

Writing is a skill. We tell our students that learning to write is like learning to play a musical instrument; the more they practice, the better they will be. *Writing from Within Intro* is designed to demonstrate to learners that they have the knowledge and ability within to develop this skill. We hope they will enjoy this text, and we look forward to hearing your comments.

Curtis Kelly
Arlen Gargagliano

Acknowledgments

Writing is a process. In this case, *Writing from Within Intro* was a process that spanned years and continents. The authors wish to thank the numerous people who helped in the development of this project. Particular thanks are owed to the following:

Thank you to the reviewers for their suggestions: Claire Chia-Hsing Pan, **Shu-te University**, Yan-chao, Taiwan; Andrew Newton, **Sogang University**, Seoul, South Korea; David Ruzicka, **Shinshu University**, Matsumoto, Japan.

The insights and suggestions of the teachers who reviewed and piloted the Writing from Within series in the initial development stages: Bruce Benson, **Shoin Women's College**, Nara, Japan; Nick Brideson, **Global Village Language Center**, Taipei, Taiwan; Martin Willis, **Tokyo Women's Christian University**, Tokyo, Japan; Sally Gearheart, **Santa Rosa Junior College**, Santa Rosa, California, USA; Michael Kastner, **Hanyang University**, Seoul, South Korea; John Hedgcock, **Monterey Institute of International Studies**, Monterey, California, USA; Chris Bunn, **City College**, San Francisco, California, USA; Kathy Sherak, **San Francisco State University**, San Francisco, California, USA.

Additional thanks are owed to the following: Fred Anderson, David Bernstein, John Gebhardt, Eileen Mckee, Lukas Murphy, Koji Nakajima, Mitsuo Nakamura, Robert Nechols, Eiji Saitou, Jeff Shaffer, Kazuko Yamasaki, Fukushi and Kokusai Communication students at Heian Jogakuin University, and especially our families, whose love and patience we continue to depend on.

The editorial and production team: Eleanor Barnes, David Bohlke, Karen Brock, Anne Garrett, Deborah Goldblatt, Louisa Hellegers, Heather McCarron, Lise Minovitz, Bill Paulk, Tami Savir, Eric Schwartz, Kayo Taguchi, Mary Vaughn, and Dorothy Zemach.

And Cambridge University Press staff and advisors: Harry Ahn, Yumiko Akeba, Kathleen Corley, Elizabeth Fuzikava, Steve Golden, Yuri Hara, Gareth Knight, Alex Lu, Alejandro Martinez, Nigel McQuitty, Carine Mitchell, Mark O'Neil, Dan Schulte, Catherine Shih, Ivan Sorrentino, Koen Van Landeghem, and Ellen Zlotnick.

Preview

Read these two examples. Which one do you think uses paragraphs? Check (✔) a or b.

a. ☐

> Last year was a big year for me.
>
> I graduated from college, I got a job in a company, and I went abroad
>
> for the first time in my life.
>
> My company sent me to Singapore to work on a new product.
>
> I enjoyed the trip, so I hope they send me again.
>
> Another big change will happen this year.
>
> I will get married this June and start living with my partner.
>
> I am looking forward to getting married, but I am a little nervous, too.

b. ☐

>   Last year was a big year for me. I graduated from college, I got a job in a company, and I went abroad for the first time in my life. My company sent me to Singapore to work on a new product. I enjoyed the trip, so I hope they send me again.
>
>   Another big change will happen this year. I will get married this June and start living with my partner. I am looking forward to getting married, but I am a little nervous, too.

If you chose b, you are right! It has two paragraphs. You will learn many things about paragraphs in this book, but for now, there are three basic rules you should know:

- *A paragraph has a special shape.*

    Start the first line of a paragraph a little to the right of the other lines. It should start about five spaces to the right. Write to the end of every line except the last one. If a sentence ends in the middle of the line, don't go down to the next line to start the next sentence. Start it on the same line.

■ *A paragraph is usually between two and seven sentences long.*

Some paragraphs are longer, and sometimes you might even see one-sentence paragraphs, but most are between two and seven sentences long.

How many sentences long is the first paragraph of example b above? Check (✔) the correct answer.

☐ *2*   ☐ *4*   ☐ *6*   ☐ *7*

■ *A paragraph is about one main idea.*

A paragraph usually explains one topic. When the topic changes, you should start a new paragraph.

Look at the first paragraph in example b on page 2. What is it about? Circle the best answer.

Singapore   *getting married*   *last year's experiences*

Look at the second paragraph in example b. What is it about? Circle the best answer.

Singapore   *getting married*   *last year's experiences*

Dear Students,

Welcome to this book! *Writing From Within Intro* will help you learn to write letters and compositions of one or two paragraphs in English. First, you will learn how to decide what to write about. Then you will learn how to write these ideas as sentences. Finally, you will learn how to organize these sentences into paragraphs.

Many of the writing topics are about things that happened or will happen in your life. We believe that "writing from within" will not only improve your writing skills, but also help you to learn about yourself.

Sincerely,
Curtis Kelly
Arlen Gargagliano

By the way, the only way to get better at writing is by practicing. You should complete all of the writing assignments in this book. We also suggest you keep a journal in a separate notebook for even more writing practice. Look for ideas to write about in your journal in each unit.

Unit 1 Who am I?

| Lesson 1 | **What is brainstorming?** | **Brainstorming** |

When you brainstorm, you write as many ideas as you can think
of about a topic. You can write words, phrases, or sentences.

words	→	*Italian, outgoing*
phrases	→	*from Rome, hate spaghetti*
sentences	→	*I'm 32 years old. I have a dog.*

1. Luigi brainstormed the topic "Who am I?" Read what he wrote.

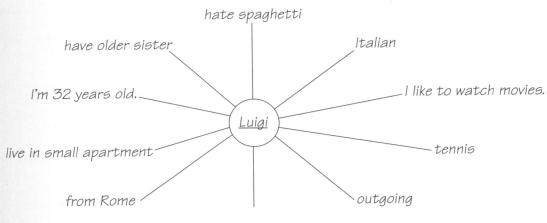

Who am I?

hate spaghetti

have older sister

Italian

I'm 32 years old.

I like to watch movies.

Luigi

live in small apartment

tennis

from Rome

outgoing

I have a dog.

2. Read Luigi's brainstorming chart again. Which picture below is Luigi?
Compare your answer with a partner.

3. Now brainstorm the topic "Who am I?" Write your name in the circle.
Then write as many words, phrases, and sentences as you can about yourself.

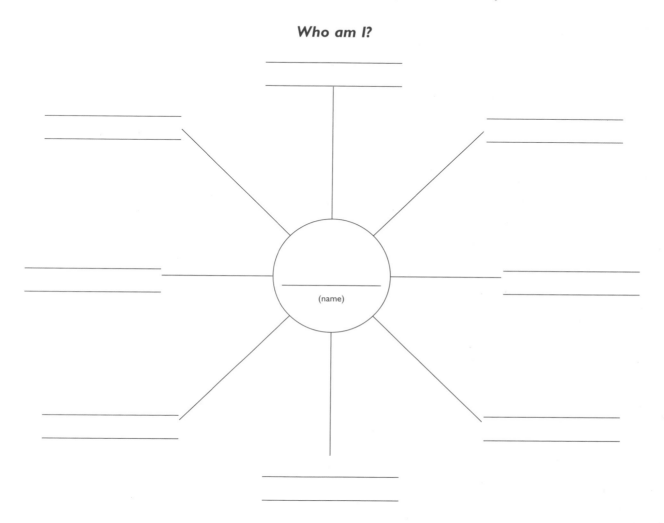

Who am I?

(name)

4. Use your information from Exercise 3 to introduce yourself to a classmate.

Hi, my name is . . .
I am . . .

Later in this unit . . .

You will write an e-mail letter of introduction.

You will also learn about topics to include in a letter of introduction.

1. Read the paragraph and follow the instructions below.

> [1] My name is Luigi. [2] I am Italian, and I am 32 years old. [3] I live in a small apartment in Rome. [4] I work in a clothing store. [5] Some day I want to be the manager. [6] Tennis is my favorite sport, but I like baseball, too.

Meaning

a. Match the sentences in the paragraph above with the topics.

☐ his job   ☐ his interests   [1] his name

☐ his age and nationality   ☐ his home   ☐ his future plans

Noticing and writing

b. Look at sentence 2 in the paragraph. Write a similar sentence with these words.

I am Spanish / I am 16 years old

_____

2. Compare answers with a partner.

Letters of introduction

When you write a letter of introduction, include information such as your name, age, gender, and nationality.

1. Read part of Maria's e-mail letter of introduction. Then write similar sentences about yourself below.

Hi there,

| **Name** | **Age** | | **Nationality** | **Gender** |
| ↓ | ↓ | | ↓ | ↓ |

My name is Maria. I am 22 years old. I am a Mexican woman. I . . .

Sincerely,
Maria

a. name: *My name is* _____

b. age: _____

c. nationality and gender: _____

2. Now write the beginning of an e-mail letter. Use your sentences from Exercise 1.

_____
(greeting)

_____

_____

_____
(closing)

_____
(your name)

Word File
Greetings
Dear _____ ,
Hello!
Hi there,

Word File
Closings
Sincerely,
Yours truly,
Best wishes,

3. Then complete your letter with a greeting and closing from the Word File.

Learning about organization

Look at the list of topics you can include in a letter of introduction.

- *family*
- *friends*
- *future plans*
- *interests*
- *likes and dislikes*
- *pets*
- *school*
- *your job*

1. Read the sentences. What is the topic of each sentence? Choose a topic from the list above. Then write a sentence about yourself.

a. I am a junior college student.

Topic: *school*

I go to a university.

b. I play in a rock band in my free time.

Topic: _____

_____

c. I want to be a pilot some day.

Topic: _____

_____

d. I work in a coffee shop after school.

Topic: _____

_____

e. I don't have a cat or dog.

Topic: _____

_____

f. My best friend is from Singapore.

Topic: _____

_____

g. I love pizza.

Topic: _____

_____

h. I have two sisters and a brother.

Topic: _____

_____

1. Read your sentences from Lesson 4 to a partner. Your partner asks for more information. Follow the examples.

A: I play in a rock band.

B: What is the name of your band?

A: Our band is called Off the Wall.

A: I play in a rock band.

B: What instrument do you play?

A: I play the guitar.

A: I am a junior college student.

B: What year are you in?

A: I am a first-year student.

A: I am a junior college student.

B: What is your major?

A: My major is biology.

2. Now write sentences for four topics you would like to include in your letter of introduction. Then write one more sentence about each topic. Follow the examples.

Sentence: _I play in a rock band._

More information: _Our band is called Off the Wall._

Sentence: _I am a junior college student._

More information: _My major is biology._

a. Sentence: _____

More information: _____

b. Sentence: _____

More information: _____

c. Sentence: _____

More information: _____

d. Sentence: _____

More information: _____

1. You are going to write a letter of introduction. First, read Lin's e-mail letter of introduction and follow the instructions below.

Dear Mr. and Mrs. Jones,

My name is Lin. I will be your homestay guest for this summer, so let me tell you about myself. I am a 24-year-old Taiwanese woman. I am studying to be a nurse at Mackay Junior College of Nursing. I live in a small apartment in Taipei, but I want to move to the countryside some day and work in a hospital. I have two younger sisters. We all get along very well. I like to dance in my free time. I take ballet lessons, but I like flamenco dancing, too. I sometimes dance at festivals.

Sincerely,

Lin

a. Circle the greeting and closing.

b. Underline the sentence that explains why Lin is writing this letter.

c. Draw a box around the sentence that tells Lin's age, nationality, and gender.

d. What other topics does Lin talk about? Check (✔) them.

☐ *her dislikes*   ☐ *her friends*   ☐ *her home*   ☐ *her job*
☐ *her family*   ☐ *her future plans*   ☐ *her interests*   ☐ *her school*

e. Lin used *Sincerely* to end her letter of introduction. Check (✔) two other ways Lin could end her letter.

☐ *Always*   ☐ *Best wishes*   ☐ *Love*   ☐ *Thank you*   ☐ *Yours truly*

2. Plan your e-mail letter of introduction.

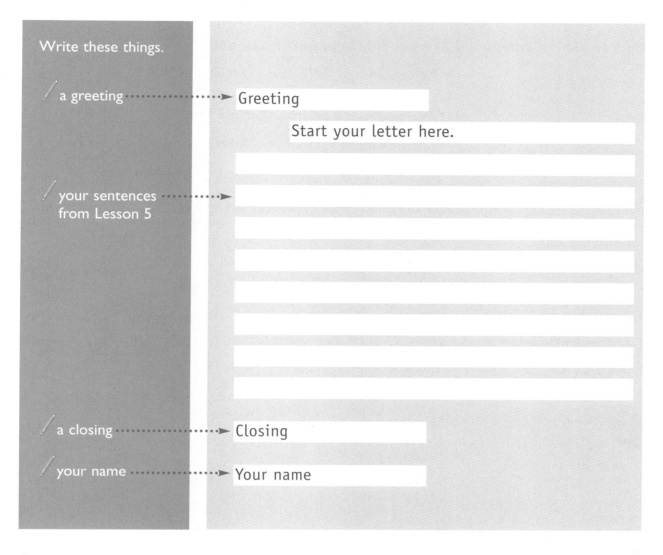

Write these things.

✓ a greeting ········► Greeting

Start your letter here.

✓ your sentences ········► from Lesson 5

✓ a closing ········► Closing

✓ your name ········► Your name

3. Now write your e-mail letter.

Writing Journal **In your journal . . .**

What do you like to do in your free time? Do you have a hobby or other special interests?

You can use and *or* but *to connect sentences. Use a comma (,) before* and *and* but *in sentences like these:*

To connect sentences with similar or additional information, use and.

I am Korean.
My family lives in Seoul.   I am Korean, **and** my family lives in Seoul.

To connect sentences with different or unexpected information, use but.

I am Korean.
My family lives in Taipei.   I am Korean, **but** my family lives in Taipei.

1. Read Carlita's e-mail letter of introduction. Circle sentences to connect with *and* or *but*.

Hi Julie,

   I will be your new roommate at Central Canadian College this fall, so let me tell you about myself. ⟨I am Mexican.⟩ ⟨I live in the United States.⟩ I have traveled a lot. I have never been to Canada. I love math and science. I want to study biology in college. In my free time, I like listening to music. I like singing. Do you like music? What kind of music do you like? Please write back to me. Tell me something about yourself.

Best wishes,
Carlita

2. Connect the circled sentences from Exercise 1 with *and* or *but*. Write them here.

a. *I am Mexican, but I live in the United States.*

b. _____

c. _____

d. _____

e. _____

3. Now look at the e-mail letter of introduction you wrote in Lesson 6. Can you connect any sentences?

Giving feedback

1. Exchange the e-mail letter of introduction you wrote in Lesson 6 with a partner. Read your partner's letter and follow the instructions below.

   a. Write your partner's greeting and closing.

   _____   _____

   b. Did your partner include these things? Check (✔) the appropriate box.

	Yes	No
Name	☐	☐
Age	☐	☐
Gender	☐	☐
Nationality	☐	☐

   c. Write the topics your partner wrote about.

   _____   _____   _____   _____

   d. Did your partner write any sentences with *and* or *but?* Write them here.

   _____

   _____

   _____

   _____

2. Write a short letter to your partner. Write something you like and a question you have.

Hi Sung-Jae,
    I like your e-mail letter. You said your English name is Jay. How did you get that name?

Best wishes,
Anna

3. Show your letter to your partner.

1. You are going to write your address in English. Look at the examples.
Then write your address below.

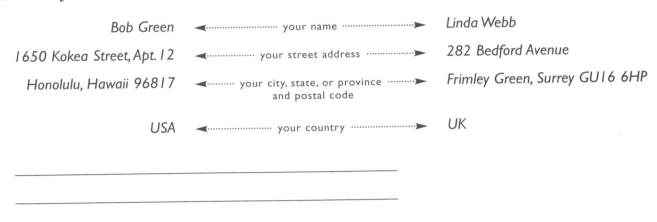

Bob Green	◄······· your name ·······►	Linda Webb
1650 Kokea Street, Apt. 12	◄······· your street address ·······►	282 Bedford Avenue
Honolulu, Hawaii 96817	◄······· your city, state, or province and postal code ·······►	Frimley Green, Surrey GU16 6HP
USA	◄······· your country ·······►	UK

_____

_____

_____

_____

2. When you write a letter, sign your name at the bottom.
Look at the examples and practice your signature three times.

Signature   **Your signature**

Minako Inomata

Minako Inomata   _____

Matthew Clark

Matthew Clark   _____

          _____

3. An e-mail signature does not contain a real signature. Look at the example and
write your e-mail signature.

E-mail signature   **Your e-mail signature**

David Ko
dko@cambridge.org
Cambridge University Press
40 West 20th Street
New York, NY 10011
(telephone) 212-555-5000

4. Now copy your letter from Lesson 6 with your address and signature.

Unit 2 special places

1. Label the picture with words from the box. Then compare answers with a partner.

☑ **the candy store**   ☐ **my best friend's house**   ☐ **the park**
☐ **the playground**   ☐ **the river**   ☐ **the school**

a. _____

b. _____

c. _____

d. _the candy store_

e. _____

f. _____

2. What are some special places near your home? What important or interesting things happened to you there in the past? Brainstorm and make two lists.

Special places	What happened
river	I fell in.

3. Compare your lists with a partner. Can you add more places to your list?

Later in this unit . . .

You will write about a special place from your childhood and what happened to you there.

You will also learn how to set the scene and write an ending to a personal story.

1. Read the paragraph and follow the instructions below.

> [1] *There was a river near my home.* [2] *One day when I was five, I was playing by the river with my friends.* [3] *I got too close to the river.* [4] *I fell in.* [5] *My clothes got wet and dirty.* [6] *When I got home, my mother was angry.*

Meaning

a. Check (✔) the topic of the paragraph above.

☐ childhood friends

☐ my mother

☐ falling in a river

Noticing and writing

b. Look at sentence 1 in the paragraph. Write a similar sentence with these words.

park / next to / my school

_____

c. Look at sentence 6 in the paragraph. Write a similar sentence with these words.

arrived at school / teacher / happy

_____

2. Compare answers with a partner.

Setting the scene

Describing where and when something happened can help set the scene.

Sentence: *There was a river.*
Sentence: *I was playing by the river.*

Where? *There was a river **near my home**.*
When? ***One day when I was five**,*
I was playing by the river.

1. Where are these places? Complete the sentences below with words from the Word File.

a. There was a park <u>next to</u> the river.

b. There was a river _____ my apartment and the train station.

c. There was a store _____ the park.

d. The store was _____ the school.

Word File
- [ ] behind
- [ ] between
- [ ] in front of
- [✔] next to

2. When did this happen? Complete the sentences with words from the Word File.

a. <u>When I was</u> in high school, I learned how to drive a car.

b. _____ , I didn't want to go to school. My friend and I drove to the beach instead.

c. We stayed at the beach _____ everyone was studying at school.

d. _____ , another friend called. She said that someone's parent had seen us at the beach.

Word File
- [ ] after school
- [ ] one day
- [✔] when I was
- [ ] while

1. Look again at your brainstorming list from Lesson 1. Choose a special place near your home where something important or interesting happened to you. Write it here.

_____

2. Look at Louis's notes about his special place. Then complete the chart about your special place.

The special place
near my school
_____

When did something important or interesting happen?

- when I was a junior high school student
- after baseball practice one day

What happened?

- I was sitting under the tree.
- I threw my cap at a bird.
- The cap got stuck.
- I threw my glove.
- My glove got stuck.
- I . . .

The special place
_____

When did something important or interesting happen?

What happened?

3. Work in groups of three. Take turns telling each other about your special place. Ask questions like these.

- What is your special place?
- When did something important or interesting happen?
- What happened there?

The ending of a personal story is important because it tells the outcome of the story and the writer's feelings.

The outcome → *After I received my prize, my mother made me a cake.*

The writer's feelings → *I was proud and happy.*

1. Look at the pictures. Complete the personal stories below with information from the box.

☐ *my father was angry*	☐ *embarrassed*
☐ *my best friend bought me a new one*	☑ *happy*
☑ *everyone cheered*	☐ *proud*

a. After my team received the trophy,
_____ *everyone cheered* _____ .

We were _____ .

b. After I lost my favorite bracelet,

_____ .

I was _____ *happy* _____ .

c. After I broke the vase,

_____ .

I was _____ .

2. Now use your information from Lesson 4 to write an ending to your own story.

_____

_____

1. You are going to write about a special place and what happened there. First, read Louis's story and follow the instructions below.

Next to my school there was an old tree. One day when I was a junior high school student, I was sitting under the tree after baseball practice. There was a bird in the tree, and I threw my cap at it. The bird flew away, but my cap got stuck in the tree. I threw my baseball glove at the cap, but my glove got stuck. When I threw my bat at the glove, it got stuck, too. Finally, I threw my ball at the bat, and even the ball got stuck. After I told my coach about the tree, he laughed and said, "That tree plays baseball better than you do." I was very embarrassed, and my face turned red.

a. Underline the sentence that tells what and where the special place was.

b. Put a star (★) above the phrase that tells when the story happened.

c. Put a check (✔) above the words that join two sentences.

d. Circle the sentence that tells the outcome.

e. Draw a box around the sentence that tells the writer's feeling.

2. Plan your paragraph about your special place and what happened there.

    a. First, draw a simple picture or a map of your special place.

    b. Write these things for your paragraph.

       / where the special place was

       _____

       / when something important or interesting happened

       _____

       / what happened (Remember to use words such as *and* and *but*.)

       _____

       _____

       / the ending

       _____

       _____

3. Now write your paragraph about your special place and what happened there.

In your journal . . .

Write about one of your favorite places. What do you do there? How often do you go there?

The prepositions in, on, and at are often used in phrases to refer to places.

1. Look at the picture. Then complete the paragraph with prepositional phrases from the box.

| ☐ **at school** | ☑ **in Australia** | ☐ **in the park** | ☐ **on a bicycle** |
| ☐ **at the end of our street** | ☐ **in a small town** | ☐ **on a bench** | ☐ **on the sidewalk** |

When I was ten years old, my family and I spent a year _____*in Australia*_____ . We lived _____ called Steele. Something interesting happened there that makes me laugh even today. My brother and I went to a small school _____ . One day _____ when we were sitting _____ in the schoolyard, my brother started laughing, and said, "Look over there! There's a kangaroo." A kangaroo was lying in front of the bus stop _____ . It was trying to keep cool in the shade. Just then a man _____ rode by. The man was riding in the street, but he was so surprised that he fell off of the bicycle. He fell on top of the kangaroo. The kangaroo jumped up and hopped away toward the park. Then the kangaroo lay down under some trees _____ and fell asleep.

2. Now look at the paragraph you wrote in Lesson 6. Can you add any prepositional phrases?

What do you think?

1. Exchange the paragraph you wrote in Lesson 6 with a partner.
Read your partner's paragraph and follow the instructions below.

a. Write answers to these questions about your partner's paragraph.

▪ Where was the special place? _____

▪ When did something important happen? _____

_____

▪ What happened? _____

_____

▪ What was the ending? _____

_____

b. Circle the words that describe the paragraph. You can write
your own words.

funny	*sad*	_____
interesting	*scary*	_____

2. Write a short letter to your partner. Ask your partner any questions you have.

Dear Isha,

    I liked reading your story.
I also fell off my bicycle when
I was in high school. Was your
bicycle damaged?

Sincerely,

Tanawan

3. Show your letter to your partner.

1. You are going to make a tourist guidebook for your town. Work in small groups. Decide whether you will make a guidebook for children, teenagers, or adults. Check (✔) your selection and write three interesting things to do.

☐ *Children*

feed the ducks in the pond

a. _____

b. _____

c. _____

☐ *Teenagers*

go shopping at the mall

a. _____

b. _____

c. _____

☐ *Adults*

go to Joe's Coffee Shop

a. _____

b. _____

c. _____

2. Now write sentences like these using your information.

Be sure to visit the pond in City Park. There are lots of fun things to do there. You can feed the ducks or go swimming. You can also buy an ice cream cone.

3. To make your guidebook, fold a piece of paper in half. Make a title page. Use the other three pages to write about the interesting things to do. Include pictures and a map.

4. When you finish, share your tourist guidebook with your classmates.

An ideal partner

Characteristics of a partner

Brainstorming

1. What characteristics are important in an ideal partner? Check (✔) them.

☐ *is rich*

☐ *has a car*

☐ *wears nice clothes*

☐ *is good-looking*

☐ *is romantic*

☐ *doesn't worry about time*

2. What five characteristics are the most important to you? Brainstorm and make a list.

 Characteristics of an ideal partner

doesn't worry about time

3. Compare your list with a partner. Can you add more characteristics to your list?

Later in this unit . . .

You will write about your ideal partner.

You will also learn how to put information in order and give reasons.

1. Read the paragraph and follow the instructions below.

[1] *What kind of partner do I want?*
★
[2] *First, I want a partner who can speak English.* [3] *Second, I want a partner who likes to go to parties because I am very outgoing.* [4] *Third, I would like someone who likes to travel.*

Meaning

a. Put a star (★) above the words that show how to put information in order.

b. Put a check (✔) above the phrase that tells why the writer wants a partner who likes to go to parties.

Noticing and writing

c. Look at sentence 2 in the paragraph. Write a similar sentence with these words.

First / want a partner / likes animals

_____

_____

d. Look at sentence 4 in the paragraph. Write a similar sentence with these words.

Third / someone / can play tennis

_____

_____

2. Compare answers with a partner.

Ideal partner interview

1. Interview your classmate about which characteristics are most important in an ideal partner. Follow the example. When you are interviewed, check (✔) *your* answers in the chart.

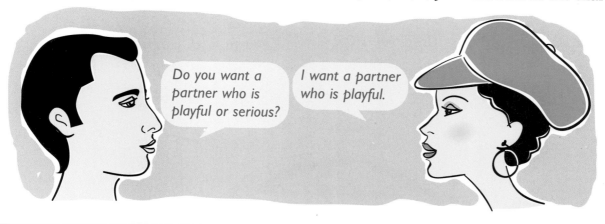

Do you want a partner who is playful or serious?

I want a partner who is playful.

	Do you want a partner who . . . ?		
		not sure or don't care	
a.	is playful ☐	☐	☐ is serious
b.	is talkative ☐	☐	☐ is quiet
c.	is good-looking ☐	☐	☐ has a great personality
d.	likes sports ☐	☐	☐ likes to study
e.	is adventurous ☐	☐	☐ is careful
f.	is passionate ☐	☐	☐ is calm
g.	likes to be alone ☐	☐	☐ doesn't like to be alone
h.	thinks money is important ☐	☐	☐ thinks an interesting life is important
i.	likes change ☐	☐	☐ doesn't like change
j.	cares about fashion ☐	☐	☐ doesn't care about fashion

2. Take turns asking a classmate, "What are three characteristics you want in an ideal partner?" Then complete the sentence with *your* answer.

I want a partner who _____ , _____ ,

and _____ .

Putting information in order

You can use words such as First, Second, and Third to put information in order.

1. Read the sentences. Then write *First, Second,* and *Third* in the correct place.

First,

What kind of partner do I want? ↑ I want a partner who has a car. I would

like a partner who doesn't have pets. I don't like pets. I would like a partner who

comes from a different country. I would like to live abroad some day.

2. Write the three most important characteristics for your ideal partner from the interview in Lesson 3. Then write a sentence about each one.

Characteristics	*Sentences*
is adventurous	*I want a partner who is adventurous.*
_____	I want _____ .
_____	I would like _____ .
_____	I would like _____ .

3. Now rewrite your sentences from Exercise 2. Write *First, Second,* and *Third* to put the information in order.

_____

_____

_____

Learning about organization

*Use **because** to give reasons in your writing.*

I want a partner who is tall.
I am tall.   →   *I want a partner who is tall **because** I am tall.*

1. Rewrite these sentences using *because*.

   a. I want a partner who cares about fashion. I like to wear nice clothes.

   _____

   _____

   b. I would like a partner who likes sports. I play tennis a lot.

   _____

   _____

   c. I would like a partner who doesn't tell lies. I had a partner once who lied

   to me and hurt me.

   _____

   _____

   d. I want a partner who likes children. I want to have a big family.

   _____

   _____

2. Write reasons for the three sentences you wrote in Lesson 4, Exercise 2.
   Use *because*.

   I want a partner who is adventurous because I like discovering new things.

   a. _____

   _____

   b. _____

   _____

   c. _____

   _____

1. You are going to write about your ideal partner. First, read Emily's paragraph and follow the instructions below.

What kind of partner do I want?
★
First, I would like a partner who likes
sports because I like to be active.
I'd rather play tennis or jog than stay at
home and watch TV all day. Second, I
want a partner who likes being with
groups of people because I like meeting
people. I enjoy parties with lots of people
because I usually make two or three new
friends. Third, I would like a partner who
comes from a different country. I love to
travel, and it is my dream to live abroad
some day. If my partner and I come from
different countries, we can teach each
other about our cultures.

a. Put a star (★) above the words Emily uses to put her ideas in order.

b. Circle the phrases that tell the three characteristics Emily wants in a partner.

c. Check (✔) the words below that Emily uses in her paragraph to write about her ideal partner.

☐ *have to*   ☐ *love*   ☐ *need*   ☐ *prefer*   ☐ *want*   ☐ *would like*

2. Plan your paragraph about your ideal partner.

Write these things.

the first sentence of the model on page 30

_____

three words to put information in order

_____   _____   _____

three characteristics of your partner

_____   _____   _____

three reasons to support the characteristics you chose

_____

_____

_____

_____

_____

_____

3. Now write your paragraph about your ideal partner.

In your journal . . .

Write a story about an ideal day with your ideal partner.

Think of
- ideal places to go
- ideal things to do
- an ideal meal
- an ideal moment

Parallel structure

You can combine sentences with similar structures.

I want a partner **who is** hardworking.
I want a partner **who is** successful.   → I want a partner **who is** hardworking and successful.

My ideal partner **likes** meeting people.
My ideal partner **likes** going to parties.   → My ideal partner **likes** meeting people and going to parties.

Note: Find words that are the same in both sentences and combine them.

1. Read the paragraph. Underline sentences that you can combine.

First, I want a partner who does water sports. I like swimming.

I also like sailing. Second, I don't like going to parties. I prefer staying at

home. I prefer being alone with my partner. I like watching TV with my

partner. I also like listening to music with my partner. Third, I hope my

partner is quiet. I also hope my partner is a good listener.

2. Combine the sentences that you underlined. Make the sentences as short as possible.

a. I like swimming and sailing.

b. _____

c. _____

d. _____

3. Now look at the paragraph you wrote in Lesson 6. Are there any sentences you can combine?

1. Exchange the paragraph you wrote in Lesson 6 with a classmate. Read your classmate's paragraph and follow the instructions below.

   a. Check (✔) the sentences that are true.

      ☐ The paragraph begins with "What kind of partner do I want?"

      ☐ There are three characteristics of an ideal partner.

      ☐ There is a reason to support each characteristic.

   b. Write the three characteristics your classmate wrote about.

   _____ _____ _____

   c. Look at the pictures. Check (✔) the ideal partner for your classmate. You can write your own idea.

☐ **artist**
has interesting ideas

☐ **college professor**
travels a lot

☐ **company president**
rich, loves to work

☐ _____

2. Write a short letter to your classmate. Write your ideas about his or her ideal partner.

Dear Nicole,

    I think I know someone who would be a good partner for you. I read your paragraph and think my friend Brian is a perfect match for you. He likes volleyball, too.

Yours truly,

Ming

3. Show your letter to your classmate.

1. You are going to create characters to take part in a dating game. Half of the class creates male characters and half creates female characters. Work alone or with a partner, and follow the instructions.

On a separate piece of paper:

a. Write a **name** for your character.

b. Draw his or her picture.

c. Write your character's **information**: name, age, gender, and nationality.

d. Write at least four **characteristics** for your character. Use ideas from Lesson 3 or your own ideas.

Name
_____

Information
_____
_____

Characteristics
_____
_____
_____

2. Now play the dating game.

FEMALE

MALE

a. Place the male and female characters in rows across from each other.

b. Read the description of your character out loud. Have classmates ask questions about your character.

c. After all of the descriptions have been read, secretly write the name of another character that best matches yours.

3. Share your matches. If two characters choose each other, they become a couple!

Brainstorming

1. Look at the photo album. Do you have similar photos? Check (✔) the ones you have.

☐ *my best friend*   ☐ *my pet*   ☐ *my first day of school*

☐ *a sports team I was on*   ☐ *my parents' wedding*   ☐ *my birthday party*

2. What are some other photos that you have? Brainstorm and make a list.

<u>I have photos of . . .</u>

my classmates and me on a school trip
my family vacation
the first time I saw my baby brother

3. Compare your list with a partner. Can you add more photos to your list?

Later in this unit . . .

You will write about one of your favorite photos.

You will also learn how to begin and end your paragraph.

1. Read the paragraph and follow the instructions below.

[1] *My favorite photo is of my friends and me
on my 21st birthday.* [2] *It was taken last year
at a restaurant.* [3] *My friends gave me some
cards and presents and sang "Happy Birthday."*
[4] *I like the photo because it reminds me of
how much I love my friends.*

Meaning

a. Put a star (★) above the phrases that tell who is in the photo
and when it was taken.

b. Underline the sentence that tells why this photo is important
to the writer.

Noticing and writing

c. Look at sentence 1 in the paragraph. Write a similar sentence with these words.

favorite photo / my family and me / New Year's Day

_____

_____

d. Look at sentence 4 in the paragraph. Write a similar sentence with these words.

like the photo / reminds me of / my family

_____

_____

2. Compare answers with a partner.

When you write about a photo, begin by describing general information about the photo.

General information usually tells who is in the photo and when the photo was taken.

My favorite photo is of my kitten on the day we got her.
My favorite photo was taken on the day we got our kitten.

1. Look at the photos. Then check (✔) the best sentence that describes each one and gives general information.

a

☐ My favorite photo was taken the day my brother and I went to Water World.

☐ My favorite photo is of my brother and me.

☐ My favorite photo was taken at Water World.

b

☐ My favorite photo is on my table next to my bed.

☐ My favorite photo is of my parents on their wedding day.

☐ My favorite photo was taken five years ago.

c

☐ My favorite photo is of my soccer team and me.

☐ My favorite photo was taken when my soccer team won the championship.

☐ My favorite photo is of the World Cup soccer tournament.

2. Look again at your brainstorming list from Lesson 1. Choose one of your favorite photos to write about. Then write a sentence about your photo that gives general information.

_____

1. Look at Nina's chart. Then complete the chart below for the photo you chose in Lesson 3.

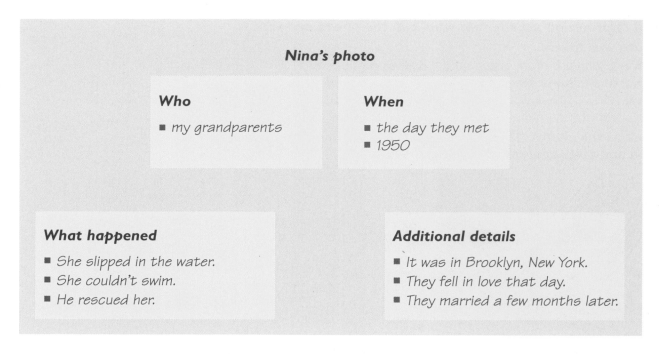

Nina's photo

Who
- my grandparents

When
- the day they met
- 1950

What happened
- She slipped in the water.
- She couldn't swim.
- He rescued her.

Additional details
- It was in Brooklyn, New York.
- They fell in love that day.
- They married a few months later.

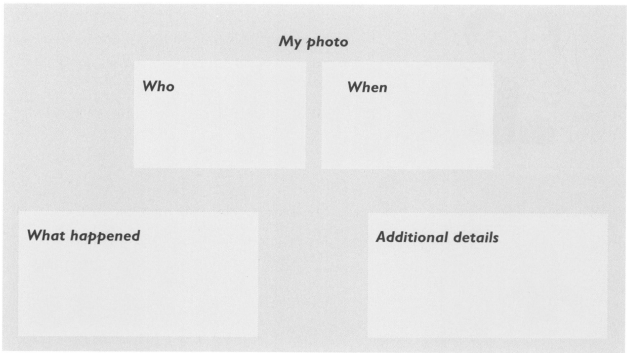

My photo

Who

When

What happened

Additional details

2. Show your chart to a partner. Is there anything you want to change or add?

Writing a concluding sentence

Learning about organization

*A concluding sentence ends a paragraph. In a paragraph about a photo,
the concluding sentence often tells why the photo is important to the writer.*

a special time in my life	→	*The photo reminds me of my childhood.*
special people or places	→	*I like the photo because it is of my best friend.*
an event	→	*The photo helps me remember the day I got my puppy.*

1. Read the groups of sentences. Check (✔) the best concluding sentence in each group.

a
- ☐ The Grand Canyon is in Arizona.
- ☑ This photo helps me remember our trip to the Grand Canyon.
- ☐ It took us six hours to hike down the trail!

b
- ☐ This photo was taken during my winter vacation.
- ☐ After we went inside, we had some hot tea.
- ☐ This photo reminds me of the first time I saw snow.

c
- ☐ When I look at this photo, I remember our wonderful play.
- ☐ I'm glad I didn't forget what to say.
- ☐ I was very nervous during the first performance.

d
- ☐ I remember that it was very hot and humid.
- ☐ This photo was taken the day we visited a big castle.
- ☐ I like this photo because it helps me remember the years I lived in Japan.

2. Now write a concluding sentence for the photo you chose in Lesson 3.

_____

1. You are going to write about your favorite photo. First, read about Nina's photo and follow the instructions below.

My favorite photo is of my grandparents on the day they met. It was taken in 1950 at the beach in Brooklyn, New York. They were both smiling because my grandfather rescued my grandmother from the ocean. She was standing in the water and slipped. She couldn't swim, so he picked her up and brought her to shore. I think that was the day they fell in love. A few months later, they got married. This photo is special to me because it helps me remember my grandparents. It also reminds me that sometimes when something unlucky happens, good people meet each other.

a. Underline the sentences that tell who is in the photo and when it was taken.

b. Circle the sentences that tell why the photo is important to Nina.

c. Put a box around the sentences that tell what happened on the day the photo was taken.

2. Now write about your photo.

Remember to write:

/ general information that introduces your photo

/ what happened and additional details (Use your chart from Lesson 4.)

/ a concluding sentence that tells why the photo is important to you

My Writing Journal

In your journal . . .

Write about taking pictures. Do you have a camera? Do you like taking pictures? What kind of pictures do you take?

*The sentence that introduces a photo is usually in the **present tense**.*
   *My favorite photo **is** of me at my first swimming lesson.*

*Sentences that give more information about the photo are
usually in the **past tense**.*
   *I **was** afraid to get into the water. My mother **had to** help me. The water **seemed** so cold!
My instructor **was** very nice, and she **helped** me relax.*

*The concluding sentence is usually in the **present tense**, too.*
   *This photo **reminds** me of that scary day.*

1. Complete the paragraph below. Choose the correct verb form.

My favorite photo _____is_____ (be) of me
and my family in Egypt. We _____ (take)
a trip to the Temple of Karnak in Luxor
a few years ago. One day, my brother and
I _____ (walk) around a temple.
We _____ (pretend) we were in a James
Bond movie and _____ (hide) from
the guards. It _____ (be) so fun.
I _____ (ask) one of the guards to take
our picture. This photo _____ (remind)
me of our spy game in that exotic place.
Whenever I see that photo, I _____ (smile).

2. Now look at the paragraph you wrote in Lesson 6. Did you use the past
tense to talk about what happened in the photo? Did you use the present tense
to talk about the photo itself?

1. Exchange the paragraph you wrote in Lesson 6 with a partner.
Read your partner's paragraph and follow the instructions below.

   a. Circle the words that describe your partner's photo. You can write
   your own words.

beautiful	*exciting*	*interesting*	*unusual*	_____
cute	*funny*	*strange*	*warm*	_____

   b. Did your partner answer these questions? Check (✔) the appropriate box.

	Yes	No
Who is in the photo?	☐	☐
When was the photo taken?	☐	☐
What were the people in the photo doing?	☐	☐
What happened that day?	☐	☐
Why is the photo important to the writer?	☐	☐

2. Write a short letter to your partner. Write something you like and a question
you have.

Dear Fernando,

   I really like your paragraph and the
photo. Everyone looks so happy! I have
one question. Are you still good friends
with the people in the picture?

Best,

Leo

3. Show your letter to your partner.

1. You are going to make a picture time line of your life. Look at the example.

| Age | 0 | 4 | 7 | 17 | 17 ½ | 21 | now |

birthday | first day of school | in Taipei | soccer champ | broken leg | met Lynn | college

2. Now write five of your important life experiences in the chart. Write how old you were. Be sure to write what you are doing now.

Important experiences	Your age
▪ I was born.	▪ 0 years old
▪	▪
▪	▪
▪	▪
▪	▪
▪	▪

3. Draw a picture or bring a photo of each experience to class. Put the pictures or photos on a big piece of paper as a time line. Write your age for each.

4. Below each picture or photo, write what happened. Follow the example.

5. Explain your time line to the class. What new things did you learn about your classmates?

Broken Leg!

I had a bicycle accident while I was riding to school for a soccer match. I was at home for a week, and all of my friends came to visit me. I could not play soccer for the rest of that year.

Unit 5 My seal

1. Here is a seal from an international high school. What does each symbol on the seal represent? Complete the sentences with words from the box.

☐ *many cultures together*   ☐ *sports*   ☑ *strength*   ☐ *study*

a. The tiger represents _____strength_____ .

b. The books represent _____ .

c. The ball and racket represent _____ .

d. The hands represent _____ .

2. Now brainstorm words and expressions that represent you. Complete the lists.

My favorite activities	My experiences	My personality	My favorite foods
surfing	trip to Paris	friendly	spaghetti

3. Compare your lists with a partner. Can you add more words and expressions to your lists?

Later in this unit . . .

You will design and write about your own seal.

You will also learn how to write topic sentences.

Three symbols

1. Read the paragraph and follow the instructions below.

> [1] *My seal has two symbols: a guitar and four stars.* [2] *There is a guitar in the center of my seal.* [3] *The guitar represents my hobby – playing rock music.* [4] *There are four stars above the guitar.* [5] *They represent my four best friends.*

Meaning

a. Write the two symbols for the seal above. Then write what the symbols represent.

Symbols   **What the symbols represent**

_____ = _____

_____ = _____

Noticing and writing

b. Look at sentence 1 in the paragraph. Write a similar sentence with these words.

seal / three symbols / pen, rose, and two hearts

_____

_____

c. Look at sentence 3 in the paragraph. Write a similar sentence with these words.

pen / my dream / becoming a writer

_____

_____

2. Compare answers with a partner.

1. Which plant or animal best represents your character? Why?
Look at the examples. Then complete the chart.

Plant or Animal	Reasons
a plant: a cactus 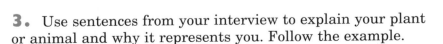	1. A cactus is strong. 2. A cactus can live without water.
an animal: a puppy	1. A puppy is playful. 2. A puppy is friendly to everyone.
_____	1. _____ 2. _____

2. Now interview a partner. Why did your partner choose the plant
or animal? Follow the example.

A: A cactus represents my character because a cactus is
strong and can live without water.

B: Why did you choose it?

A: I want to be a person who is strong. I want to be a person
who doesn't need much money or expensive clothes.

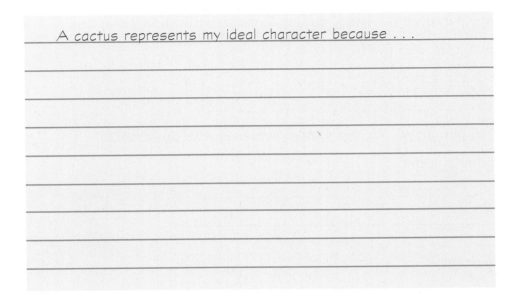

3. Use sentences from your interview to explain your plant
or animal and why it represents you. Follow the example.

A cactus represents my ideal character because . . .

_____

_____

_____

_____

_____

_____

_____

_____

_____

Designing a seal

1. Look at Ruby's seal, and then design your own seal. Follow the instructions.

   a. Choose the plant or animal from Lesson 3 for the center of your seal and draw it on your seal.

   b. Look again at your brainstorming lists from Lesson 1. Choose at least two other words or expressions to represent you. Draw the symbols on your seal.

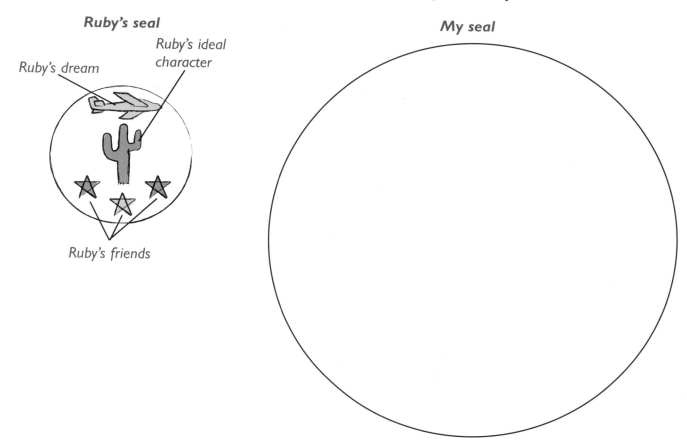

Ruby's seal

Ruby's ideal character

Ruby's dream

Ruby's friends

My seal

2. Look at Ruby's seal. Where are the symbols? Complete the sentences with words from the Word File.

   a. There is a cactus _____ of Ruby's seal.

   b. _____ the cactus there are stars.

   c. There is a plane _____ the cactus.

Word File
- [ ] above
- [ ] below
- [ ] in the center

3. Where are the symbols on your seal? Write sentences.

   a. _____

   b. _____

   c. _____

A topic sentence *is useful for organizing a paragraph. It tells the subject of the paragraph and gives a main idea or opinion.*

> **topic sentence:** *The apple has been a symbol of many things.*
>
> **topic sentence:** *Symbols can represent different things in different cultures.*

1. Here are sentences from a paragraph about famous symbols. Complete the sentences with words from the box.

☐ **the royal family**   ☐ **a hospital**   ☐ **knowledge**   ☐ **good luck**   ☑ **the Queen**

In England, a red rose 🌹 represents ___the Queen___ . In Germany, an apple 🍎 represents _____ . In Japan, a chrysanthemum ⚙ represents _____ . In the United States, an "H" **H** represents _____ . In China, the number eight **8** represents _____ .

2. The paragraph in Exercise 1 has no topic sentence. Check (✔) the best topic sentence for the paragraph.

☐ Flowers represent the rulers of countries.

☐ There are many different symbols around the world.

☐ The red rose is the most beautiful symbol.

3. Check (✔) the best topic sentence for a paragraph about Ruby's seal in Lesson 4.

☐ I am going to write about my seal.

☐ The cactus is my favorite symbol.

☐ My seal has three symbols: a cactus, stars, and an airplane.

4. Now write a topic sentence for a paragraph about your seal.

_____

1. You are going to write about your personal seal. First, read about Manuel's seal and follow the instructions below.

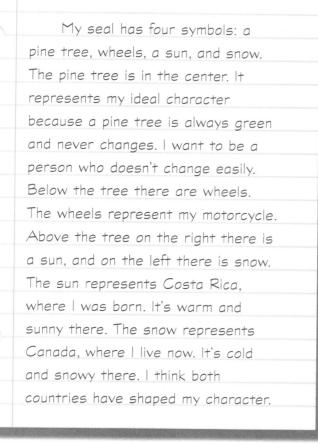

My seal has four symbols: a pine tree, wheels, a sun, and snow. The pine tree is in the center. It represents my ideal character because a pine tree is always green and never changes. I want to be a person who doesn't change easily. Below the tree there are wheels. The wheels represent my motorcycle. Above the tree on the right there is a sun, and on the left there is snow. The sun represents Costa Rica, where I was born. It's warm and sunny there. The snow represents Canada, where I live now. It's cold and snowy there. I think both countries have shaped my character.

a. Underline the topic sentence.

b. Put a star (★) above the phrases that tell where the symbols on the seal are located.

c. Write the four symbols and what they represent.

Symbol 1: _____ *pine tree* _____
 a character that never changes

Symbol 2: _____

_____

Symbol 3: _____

_____

Symbol 4: _____

_____

2. Now write about your personal seal. Draw the seal at the top of your paper. Then write about your seal below it.

Remember to write:

✓ a topic sentence

✓ a description of the main symbol in the center: a plant or animal

✓ a description of the other symbols on your seal

✓ what each symbol represents

In your journal . . .

Write about the colors you could include on your seal. Explain what each color means. For example, "Blue represents my home and family because the roof on our house is blue."

Commas with *because*

In Unit 3 you learned to connect sentences with because to give reasons.

*A pine tree represents my ideal character **because** it is always green and never changes.*

Because *can also come at the beginning of a sentence. Note the use of the comma.*

***Because** a pine tree is always green and never changes, it represents my ideal character.*

1. Rewrite these sentences. Make sure *because* explains the reason.

   a. My seal has musical notes around the edge. I love singing.

   Because <u>I love singing, my seal has musical notes around the edge</u> .

   b. The gold coin represents my father. He always gives me money.

   _____ because _____ .

   c. I am small and strong. I chose an ant to represent myself.

   Because _____ .

   d. I love plants and trees. The main color of my seal is green.

   Because _____ .

   e. I drew ocean waves at the bottom. My hobby is sailing.

   Because _____ .

   f. My best friend drew my seal. I'm very bad at drawing.

   _____ because _____ .

   g. A rabbit represents my character. A rabbit is quiet and friendly.

   _____ because _____ .

   h. The bird represents my school baseball team. We are called the Eagles.

   _____ because _____ .

   i. There is a piano in the center of my seal. Music is the most important thing in my life.

   Because _____ .

   j. I like painting. There are many colors in my seal.

   _____ because _____ .

2. Now look at the paragraph you wrote in Lesson 6. Are there any sentences with *because*? Can you change the position of *because* in some of them?

1. Work in groups of four. Exchange the paragraphs you wrote in Lesson 6 with members of another group. Read all of the other group's paragraphs and complete the chart.

Which seal . . . ?	
. . . surprised you the most	
. . . had the most interesting design	
. . . had the most unusual symbol	
. . . was easiest to understand	

2. Choose one paragraph to give feedback on. Write the symbols and what they represent.

Group member's name: _____

Symbols	What the symbols represent
1. _____	_____
2. _____	_____
3. _____	_____

3. Check (✔) the appropriate sentences about the paragraph you chose in Exercise 2.

☐ The paragraph has a topic sentence.   ☐ The symbols are explained clearly.

☐ There is a plant or animal in the seal.   ☐ The ideas are interesting.

☐ The paragraph explains where the symbols are.   ☐ The paragraph needs more explanation.

4. Write a short letter to your classmate. Write your comments or questions about the seal.

Dear Catherine,

   I liked your seal. I think an eagle is a good symbol for you. I liked the river too, but I don't understand why the river was above the eagle. Can you tell me? Thank you.

Your classmate,
Eva

5. Show your letter to your classmate.

1. You and your classmates are going to make a group flag. Work in small groups. Choose a club or class as the subject for your flag. Circle your group's choice or write your own idea.

English class   *a hobby club*   *science class*   *a sports club* _____

2. Choose two words from the Word File to represent your club or class. You can use your own words. Then create a symbol for each word.

Words	Symbols

Word File

- [ ] athletic
- [ ] caring
- [ ] competitive
- [ ] creative
- [ ] dependable
- [ ] friendly
- [ ] hardworking
- [ ] helpful
- [ ] modern
- [ ] traditional
- [ ] _____
- [ ] _____

3. Decide on colors to represent your club or class. Write the colors and what each color represents.

Color	What it represents

English Class Flag

Blue represents the outside world.   Red represents the caring feeling in this class.

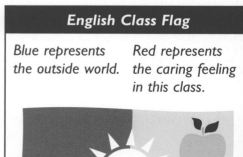

The sun in the middle represents our friendly class.   The apple represents our helpful teacher.

4. Now make a poster. Draw the flag in the middle of a big piece of paper. Write an explanation for each part.

5. Present your poster to the class.

6 *It's a party!*

Brainstorming

1. Which of these activities would you like to do with your class? Check (✔) them.

☐ *do a traditional dance*

☐ *go on a hike*

☐ *sing a song*

☐ *have a pizza party*

☐ *have everyone wear aloha shirts on the same day*

☐ *watch a movie*

2. What other activities would you like to do with your class? Brainstorm and make a list.

Class activities

have a karaoke party

3. Compare your list with a partner. Can you add more activities to your list?

Later in this unit . . .

You will write a notice and a paragraph about a class party.

You will also learn how to plan a paragraph by making a list.

1. Read the paragraph and follow the instructions below.

[1] *The end of the school year is coming, so let's go on a class hike!* [2] *The hike will start at 8:00 a.m. and end at 2:00 p.m.* [3] *Please be on time.* [4] *Wear shorts and a T-shirt because it will probably be hot.*

Meaning

a. Put a star (★) above the kind of class activity this paragraph is about.

b. Read the sentences. Check (✔) two sentences to add to the paragraph.

☐ Don't forget to bring a water bottle.

☐ Hiking is less popular than snowboarding.

☐ We won't eat dinner there.

☐ We'll meet at Bell School at 6:50 a.m.

Noticing and writing

c. Look at sentence 1 in the paragraph. Write a similar sentence with these words.

Winter is coming / class ski trip

_____

_____

d. Look at sentence 4 in the paragraph. Write a similar sentence with these words.

Bring / coat and gloves / cold

_____

_____

2. Compare answers with a partner.

1. Look at Andy's notes about a class party. Then complete his party notice below.

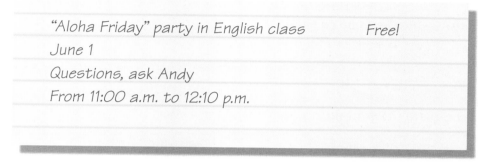

> "Aloha Friday" party in English class   Free!
> June 1
> Questions, ask Andy
> From 11:00 a.m. to 12:10 p.m.

Class party!

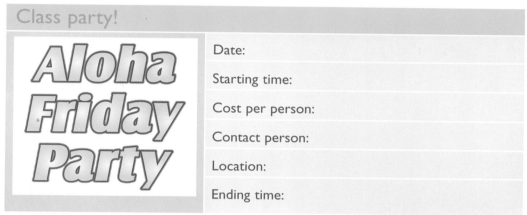

Aloha Friday Party

Date:

Starting time:

Cost per person:

Contact person:

Location:

Ending time:

2. Look again at your brainstorming list from Lesson 1. Choose an idea for a class party. Then complete the notice for your party.

Class party!

_____
(name of party)

Date:

Starting time:

Cost per person:

Contact person:

Location:

Ending time:

3. Read these topic sentences. Then write a similar topic sentence for your class party.

Summer is coming, so let's celebrate with an "Aloha Friday" party!

Let's have a karaoke party before final exams!

My topic sentence: _____

Lesson 4 — Plans and instructions

Here are examples of plans and instructions.

Plans
We will go to the Sunshine Theater.
We will listen to music.
I will play the piano.

Instructions
Please be on time.
Bring your favorite CD.
Please try to study the words to the song.

1. Look at the pictures. Then complete the sentences about plans for a class hiking party.

a We will meet at _____ *Bell School* _____ at 6:50 a.m.

b We will take a _____ to Riverview Park.

c After we get there, we will _____ along the trail to Crystal Pond.

d At Crystal Pond, we will _____ .

2. Complete the sentences with words from the Word File.

a. Please _____ *do* _____ not be late.

b. _____ something to eat and drink.

c. _____ old clothes because you will get dirty.

d. _____ all of your friends about the hike!

Word File
- [ ] bring
- [✔] do
- [ ] tell
- [ ] wear

One way to plan a paragraph is to make a list of ideas.
Write key words and phrases instead of sentences.

1. Look at Andy's list of ideas for his party. Then complete one for your party.

"Aloha Friday" Party!

Before the party	✔ tell people to wear Hawaiian clothes	buy coconuts and pineapple juice
	choose a Hawaiian song to sing	prepare fashion show prizes
At the party	✔ explain the fashion contest	✔ hold the contest
	✔ judge the contest (with Lee)	✔ serve the food and drinks
	✔ play the ukulele	✔ teach a Hawaiian song

_____
(name of party)

Before the party	
At the party	

2. Look again at Andy's list. Notice he checked (✔) the information he wanted to include in his paragraph about the party. Look again at your list and check (✔) the information you want to include in your paragraph.

3. Show your list to a partner. Is there anything you want to change or add?

1. You are going to write a notice and a paragraph about your party. First, read Andy's notice and paragraph and follow the instructions below.

"Aloha Friday" Party

Date: June 1   Starting Time: 11:00 a.m.

Location: English class   Ending Time: 12:10 p.m.

Cost per person: It's free!   Contact person: Andy

    Summer is coming, so let's celebrate with an "Aloha Friday" party! Please try to wear Hawaiian clothes to the party because we are going to have a Hawaiian fashion contest. The Hawaiian clothes can be an aloha shirt, a dress with a tropical print, or even sandals and a straw hat. At the beginning of class, each person will walk in front of the class so that we can choose the best Hawaiian look. After the contest, we will eat some coconuts and drink pineapple juice. I'll also play my ukulele and teach the class a Hawaiian song.

a. Underline the topic sentence.

b. Circle the sentence that gives an instruction.

c. Put a star (★) above the phrases that tell what the party activities will be.

d. Draw a box around the sentence that gives examples of Hawaiian clothes.

2. Plan the notice and paragraph for your class party.

    a. Write these things for your notice.

My party notice
✎ the name of the party _____
✎ the day and time _____
✎ the place _____
✎ the contact person _____
✎ the cost _____

    b. Write these things for your paragraph.

My paragraph
✎ a topic sentence to announce the party _____
_____
✎ what kind of party it will be _____
_____
✎ what activities everyone will do _____
_____
✎ a description of the activities _____
_____
✎ what people should wear or bring _____
_____

3. Now write your notice and paragraph.

In your journal . . .

Write about the best party you have ever gone to.
What kind of party was it? Where was it? What did you
do at it? Who came? What interesting things happened?

So that and to

To show a reason or purpose, combine sentences using **so that** *and* **to**.

Let's meet tomorrow morning. We can plan the party.

Let's meet tomorrow morning **so that** *we can plan the party.*

Let's meet tomorrow morning **to** *plan the party.*

1. Rewrite the sentences two ways. Use *so that* and *to*.

a. I will go to the restaurant tomorrow. I can make reservations for our party.

(so that) _____

(to) _____

b. Let's swap lunches on Tuesday. We can see what other people like to eat.

(so that) _____

(to) _____

c. I think we should go to the movie early. We can buy popcorn and drinks for everyone.

(so that) _____

(to) _____

d. Please bring a hat. You can keep from getting a sunburn.

(so that) _____

(to) _____

e. Let's meet at 6:15. We can get to the concert before it starts.

(so that) _____

(to) _____

f. Bring some money. You can rent a boat at the lake.

(so that) _____

(to) _____

2. Now look at your party proposal. Are there any sentences you could combine with *so that* or *to*?

What do you think?

1. Exchange the paragraph you wrote in Lesson 6 with a partner. Read your partner's paragraph and follow the instructions below.

a. Did your partner answer these questions? Check (✔) the appropriate box.

	Yes	No
What kind of party will it be?	☐	☐
What activities will everyone do?	☐	☐
When and where will the party be?	☐	☐
How much will the party cost?	☐	☐
What should everyone wear or bring?	☐	☐

b. Circle one or two sentences that describe your partner's party. You can write your own sentences.

It's fun.	*It's easy to do.* _____
It's unique.	*It's free.* _____

2. Write a short letter to your partner. Write your comments or questions about the party.

Dear Andy,

    I liked your idea for an "Aloha Friday" party. I think it will be fun. I have some Hawaiian leis at home. Would you like me to bring them to the party? I can't wait for "Aloha Friday"!

Cheri

3. Put all of the party ideas on desks. Then choose three parties you would like to attend and write them here.

_____ _____ _____

4. Vote on a class party!

1. You are going to design a poster for your party. Follow the instructions.

    a. Choose a word from the box or your own word that explains the mood of your party. Write it on the line below.

| crazy | elegant | exciting | exotic | friendly | quiet | traditional | unique |

    b. Read these design ideas. Then choose design ideas to use in your poster.

Color: Use colors and combinations of colors to show the theme of your party.

Position: Think carefully about where you put items on your poster.

Space: To make your message more powerful, don't put too many pictures in your poster.

Size: Make the most important information the largest.

2. Now design your poster.

3. When you finish, hang your posters up around the classroom. Which parties would you like to attend?

Thank-you letter

Things to be thankful for

Brainstorming

1. Which of these nice things has someone done for you recently? Check (✔) them.

☐ *listened to my problem*

☐ *gave me advice*

☐ *helped me go abroad*

☐ *made lunch for me*

☐ *took me to dinner*

☐ *gave me a present*

2. Who has done some nice things for you? Brainstorm and make two lists.

Who?	The nice thing
my boyfriend	gave me a ring

3. Compare lists with a partner. Can you add more to your lists?

Later in this unit . . .

You will write a thank-you letter expressing appreciation.

You will also learn how to give reasons and use time markers in a story.

1. Read the paragraph and follow the instructions below.

> [1] I am writing to thank you for the lovely gift. [2] I am sometimes late, so a clock is a perfect gift for me! [3] Also, it is just the right size for my desk. [4] Thanks so much again for the gift.

Meaning

a. Underline the sentence that explains why the writer is writing.

b. Put a star (★) above the phrases that describe why it is a good gift.

Noticing and writing

c. Look at sentence 1 in the paragraph. Write a similar sentence with these words.

writing / thank you / taking me to the concert

_____

_____

d. Look at sentence 4 in the paragraph. Write a similar sentence with these words.

Thanks / the thoughtful gift

_____

_____

2. Compare answers with a partner.

You can also use for + –ing to give a reason.

I want to thank Rachel. → She said hello to me when I was sad.
Rachel, I want to thank you **for saying** hello to me when I was sad.

I want to thank Antonio. → He helped me with my homework.
Antonio, I want to thank you **for helping** me with my homework.

1. Rewrite these sentences. Use *for + –ing*.

a. I want to thank you. You gave me a birthday party.

_____

b. I want to thank you. You showed me where the library is.

_____

c. I want to thank you. You saved me a seat in the cafeteria.

_____

2. Now thank three classmates for something nice they did. Write their names. Then complete the sentences. Use *for + –ing*.

a. Classmate: _____ I want to thank you _____ .

b. Classmate: _____ I want to thank you _____ .

c. Classmate: _____ I want to thank you _____ .

3. **Thank-you chain.** Take turns reading your sentences to the class. The person named in the sentence continues the chain.

Kenji, I want to thank you for smiling.

Someone to thank

Prewriting

1. Look at Tony's notes. Then choose someone who did something nice for you and who you would like to thank. Complete the chart below.

The person I want to thank	*Kevin*
What the person did	*He told the teacher I forgot to bring my homework to class because I was tired.*
Why I am thankful	*He understood how I felt.* *He helped me with my problem.*

The person I want to thank	
What the person did	
Why I am thankful	

2. Take turns asking a classmate these questions.

- Who is the person you want to thank?
- What nice thing did ____________ (name) do for you?
- Why are you thankful?

3. Write about why you are thankful. Begin with "Thank you so much."

Thank you so much. You understood how I felt, and you helped me with my problem.

____

____

Use time markers such as before, while, *and* after *in your writing to organize the events in your story.*

Before *I got home, my friends brought a cake to my house and put up a sign.*
While *I was unlocking the front door, they hid behind the sofa and chairs.*
After *I came in and turned on the light, all of my friends shouted, "Happy birthday."*

My Surprise Party

before *I got home* **while** *I was unlocking the door* **after** *I came in*

1. Complete the story with *before, while,* or *after.*

One evening ___*after*___ school, I walked to the bus stop. _____
I was walking, it started to rain, but I did not have an umbrella. _____
I was waiting for the bus, I got wetter and wetter. About ten minutes
_____ the bus came, an old man walked up to the bus stop. He saw
how wet I was, so he took off his jacket and gave it to me _____
we were talking. Even today, _____ so many years, I am still grateful
to that man for his kindness.

2. Look again at Lesson 4. Write three sentences about the nice thing someone did for you. Use *before, while,* and *after.*

a. _____

b. _____

c. _____

1. You are going to write a thank-you letter. First, read Tony's letter and follow the instructions below.

> Dear Kevin,
>
>   I'm writing to thank you for helping me at school one day. Before I went to school, I forgot to put my homework in my backpack. The teacher collected the homework, but I could not give her mine. While we were in class, the teacher didn't say anything, but I was worried that she thought I was a bad student. After class you told the teacher I had worked on my homework for four hours. You told her that I forgot to bring it to class because I was so tired. She smiled and asked me to bring it the next day. I know I should have told her myself, but I was too embarrassed. Thank you so much for your kindness, Kevin. You understood how I felt, and you helped me with my problem.
>
> Your friend,
> Tony

a. Underline the sentence that explains why Tony is writing the letter.

b. Put a star (★) above the time markers.

c. Tony used *Your friend* to end his letter. Check (✔) two other ways Tony could end his letter.

☐ *Best regards*   ☐ *I have to go now*   ☐ *Waiting for your reply*
☐ *Bye-bye*   ☐ *Signed*   ☐ *Yours truly*

2. Plan your thank-you letter.

Write these things.

    / your greeting (Begin with *Dear.*)

    _____

    / why you are writing this letter

    _____

    / sentences about what happened (Use *before, while,* and *after.*)

    _____

    _____

    _____

    _____

    / sentences that tell why you are thankful (Begin with *Thank you so much for . . .*)

    _____

    _____

    _____

    / a closing for your letter and your name

    _____

    _____

3. Now write your thank-you letter.

In your journal . . .

Write about a nice thing you did for someone. What was the situation? Why did you decide to do it? How did that person feel? How did you feel? Would you do it again?

Use before and after to show which event came first in a story.

Order of events

1. *I wasn't happy.*   2. *I met you.*   →   *I wasn't happy* **before** *I met you.*
1. *You lent me money.*   2. *I ate lunch.*   →   *I ate lunch* **after** *you lent me money.*

Before and after can be used at the beginning or in the middle of a sentence. Note the use of commas.

(comma)   **Before** *I met you, I wasn't happy.*
(no comma)   *I wasn't happy* **before** *I met you.*

(comma)   **After** *you lent me money, I ate lunch.*
(no comma)   *I ate lunch* **after** *you lent me money.*

1. Read the pairs of sentences. Write (1) next to the event that happened first. Write (2) next to the event that happened second. Then rewrite the sentences using *before* or *after*.

_2_ I was happy.   *I was happy after you took*

_1_ You took me to a movie.   *me to a movie.*

___ I got your advice.   _____

___ I felt better.   _____

___ You gave me a gift.   _____

___ I didn't know how kind you were.   _____

___ I listened to your advice.   _____

___ I did not know how to solve my problem.   _____

___ You heard that I was in the hospital. _____

___ You called me.   _____

2. Now look at the thank-you letter you wrote in Lesson 6. Are there any sentences with *before* or *after*? Did you use commas correctly?

1. Exchange the paragraph you wrote in Lesson 6 with a partner. Read your partner's paragraph and follow the instructions below.

a. Check (✔) the appropriate box.

Did your partner include . . . ?

	Yes	No
. . . Dear _____, name	☐	☐
. . . the reason for writing	☐	☐
. . . some details about what happened	☐	☐
. . . sentences with time markers	☐	☐
. . . a closing and a signature	☐	☐

b. Circle one or two sentences that are true. You can write your own sentence.

My partner seems kind and warmhearted.

The person my partner wrote about seems kind and warmhearted.

I want my partner to explain the letter to me.

_____

2. Write a short letter to your partner. Write something you like and a question you have.

Dear Mi-young,

    I liked your letter. You were very sincere.
You were lucky to get such a nice present!
What did you buy your friend for his birthday?

Best regards,
Anita

3. Show your letter to your partner.

1. You are going to write a letter to a foreign company whose service or product you appreciate. Look at the following illustrations.

a shop   a restaurant   a hotel

a snack food   designer jeans   a cell phone service

2. Now choose a foreign company. Use ideas from Exercise 1 or your own ideas.

a. Write the name of the company and its service or product below.

Name of company: *Sheraton Waikiki* _____

Service or product: *hotel* _____

b. Find the address of the company on the product or on the Internet.

3. Now write a letter to the company. Follow the example below.

Sheraton Waikiki Hotel

2255 Kalakaua Avenue

Honolulu, HI 96830

Dear Sir or Madam,

    I am writing to thank you for the wonderful service I received at your hotel. Everyone was very kind and helpful. While I was there, I wanted to go to Hanauma Bay. I didn't know how to go, but one of your employees showed me how to take the bus. I had a very nice tour. I am grateful for the wonderful service I received.

Sincerely,

Yuzo Murakami

---

8 Movie review

Great movies

Brainstorming

1. Do you know these movies? Match the pictures with the movie titles. Then check your answers at the bottom of the page.

a. _____ *Titanic*

b. _____ *The Lord of the Rings*

c. ___1___ *Star Wars*

d. _____ *Jurassic Park*

e. _____ *Seabiscuit*

f. _____ *Master and Commander*

2. What movies have you seen recently? Brainstorm and make a list.

 Movies

Titanic

3. Compare lists with a partner. Can you add more movies to your list?

Later in this unit . . .

You will write a movie review.

You will also learn how to summarize a movie and include an opinion.

I. Read the paragraph and follow the instructions below.

[1] *I liked the movie* The Sixth Sense *very much.* [2] *The main characters of the movie are a little boy, played by Haley Joel Osment, and a psychologist, played by Bruce Willis.* [3] *The movie is about a little boy who can see ghosts.* [4] *The main message of* The Sixth Sense *is that ghosts are not always bad.*

Meaning

a. Put a star (★) above the characters and two stars (★★) above the names of the actors.

b. Put a check (✔) above the phrase that explains what the movie is trying to say or teach the audience.

Noticing and writing

c. Look at sentence 3 in the paragraph. Write a similar sentence with these words.

Master and Commander / an English captain / fights a French ship

_____

_____

d. Look at sentence 4 in the paragraph. Write a similar sentence with these words.

main message / *Star Wars* / the good side wins

_____

_____

2. Compare answers with a partner.

Learning about organization

A movie review often begins with the summary of the movie.
The summary explains what the movie is about. It has three parts.

- **the characters and actors**
- **the plot**
- **the message**

1. Look at your brainstorming notes from Lesson 1. Then choose a movie to review and write it here.

_____

2. Read the parts of three movie reviews and follow the instructions.

The characters and actors
In Notting Hill, Hugh Grant, my favorite actor, is the owner of a bookshop in London. He falls in love with Julia Roberts, who plays an American movie star.

a. Write about the characters and actors in your movie.

_____
_____
_____
_____

The plot
Jurassic Park is a movie about a theme park full of dinosaurs. The dinosaurs get out of the park and attack a group of people.

b. Write the plot of your movie.

_____
_____
_____
_____

The message
The message of Seabiscuit is that spirit and heart are more important than size and strength. The smaller horse wins the race because he tries harder than the bigger horses.

c. Write the message of your movie.

_____
_____
_____
_____

Writing more than one paragraph

In a movie review, the second paragraph gives your opinion of the movie. In the second paragraph, you will

- *discuss the quality of the movie and the acting.*
- *finish with a recommendation.*

1. Read the movie review and divide it into two paragraphs. Draw a circle around the sentence that begins the second paragraph.

<u>Bend It Like Beckham</u> tells the story of a women's soccer team in England. Parminder Nagra plays Jess, a girl whose parents don't think girls should play professional soccer. However, Jess is very good, and she continues playing. In the end, her parents recognize her talent and understand how much she wants to play. The message of the movie is that you should follow your dream. <u>Bend It Like Beckham</u> was very entertaining. There was action, drama, romance, and humor. I thought all of the actors were very good. The characters were believable, and I could understand the feelings of both Jess and her family. I learned a lot about soccer and English culture, too. I highly recommend this movie. Even if you are not interested in sports, you will love it!

2. Read more sentences from the movie review. In which paragraph do they belong? Write (1) for paragraph 1 and (2) for paragraph 2.

a. _____ They want her to act more like other girls.

b. _____ The soccer scenes were really exciting.

c. _____ The music was also wonderful.

d. _____ At first, her parents are angry with her.

3. Think about the movie you chose in Lesson 3. Circle the word or words that describe it. You can write your own words.

boring	exciting	scary	unbelievable	_____
entertaining	funny	slow	violent	_____

1. Interview a partner.

a. Ask your partner about the movie he or she chose in Lesson 3. Ask questions like these.

Any questions?

What is the movie's plot?

Who are the main characters?

What is the message?

What roles do they play?

b. Ask your partner's opinion of the movie he or she chose in Lesson 3. Ask questions like these.

- What did you like or dislike about the movie?
- Were the actors good?
- Do you recommend this movie? Why or why not?

2. Now write your opinion of the movie you chose in Lesson 3. Follow the example.

> I think the movie <u>Finding Nemo</u> was a wonderful movie. It tells the story of a father's love for his son. At the same time, the characters were funny and cute. I recommend that you see this movie.

1. You are going to write a movie review. First, read Jun's movie review and follow the instructions below.

> Titanic is a movie about a ship that sinks. It is based on a true story that happened many years ago. The main characters are Jack and Rose, played by Leonardo DiCaprio and Kate Winslet. Jack is poor and Rose is rich. Rose's family doesn't want her to talk to Jack, but she does, and they fall in love. Sadly, the ship sinks and Jack dies. Even so, Rose remembers him for the rest of her life. The message of Titanic is that love is very powerful. We must trust our hearts.
>
> I think Titanic was a great movie. It was a sad story, but it taught me a lot about history, and also about love. I liked Jack and Rose. They were strong and trusted each other. I think everyone should see this wonderful movie.

a. Underline the topic sentence in each paragraph.

b. Put a star (★) above the names of the movie characters.

c. Which of these sentences is most similar to the movie's message? Check (✔) it.

☐ Love is everywhere.

☐ Love is strong and everlasting.

☐ Love is hard to find.

2. Now write your movie review. Remember to write:

Paragraph 1: The summary	Paragraph 2: My opinion
⁄ a topic sentence	⁄ a topic sentence
⁄ the characters	⁄ what you liked and did not like
⁄ the plot	⁄ whether you recommend the movie or not
⁄ the message	

In your journal . . .

Write about what kind of movies you like best.
Are there any kinds of movies that you don't like? Why?

To avoid repeating names, use pronouns and possessive adjectives.

subject pronouns	object pronouns	possessive adjectives
he, she, they	**him, her, them**	**his, her, their**

(not good)   Rose's family doesn't want **Rose** to talk to Jack, but **Rose** does, and **Rose and Jack** fall in love.

(better)   Rose's family doesn't want **her** to talk to Jack, but **she** does, and **they** fall in love.

1. Read the paragraph below. Underline names that you can replace. Then write a pronoun or possessive adjective above the underlined names. Do not change the **bolded** words.

> One message of the **Harry Potter** movies is that good friends are
>
> important. **Harry** has many problems in <u>Harry's</u> life. Harry is always in danger.
> *(his)*
>
> However, **Harry** solves Harry's problems because Harry has **some good friends**
>
> to help Harry. The good friends are not typical kids. The good friends know magic
>
> and have some special skills. **Harry**'s best friend is **Ron**. Ron is loyal and
>
> dependable. Ron often helps **Harry** get out of danger. **Harry**'s other good friend
>
> is **Hermione**. Hermione is very smart and good at Hermione's studies. **Hermione**
>
> helps **Harry** with Harry's homework. **Harry** depends a lot on **Ron** and **Hermione**,
>
> and Ron and Hermione help Harry through many adventures. Harry, Ron, and
>
> Hermione's friendship is one of my favorite things about the movies.

2. Now look at the movie review you wrote in Lesson 6. Are there any places where you can replace names?

What do you think?

1. Work in groups of three or four. Exchange the movie reviews you wrote in Lesson 6 with members of another group. Read all of the other group's reviews.

2. Give an award to each movie. Choose from the awards in the box or write your own idea.

| *Best Actor/Actress* | *Funniest* | *Most Original* | *Most Unbelievable* | _____ |

Name of movie	Awards

3. Now choose one movie review to give feedback on. Check (✔) the appropriate box.

	Yes	No
Does the review have two paragraphs?	☐	☐
Is the plot explained?	☐	☐
Are the characters explained?	☐	☐
Is the message explained?	☐	☐
Does the review include the writer's opinion about the movie?	☐	☐
Does the writer recommend the movie?	☐	☐

4. Write a short letter to your classmate. Write something you like and a question you have.

> Dear Sabrina,
>   I read your review of the movie Shakespeare in Love, and I liked it very much. I especially liked the way you told the plot of the movie. I saw the movie, too, and liked it very much. Do you think . . .

NOW PLAYING
Shakespeare In Love

5. Show your letter to your classmate.

6. Return the reviews to the other group members and tell them what awards their movies won. Do you agree with the award your movie won?

1. You and your classmates are going to produce a movie. Form small groups of three or four. Give your movie a name. Write it here.

_____

2. Write your ideas for the movie's plot.

3. Complete the chart. Write the names of the characters and the actors.

Characters	Actors

The New Snow White

Starring: _Kate Hudson and Susan Sarandon_

Kate Hudson plays Snow White and Susan Sarandon plays the evil stepmother. When the stepmother asks her magic mirror who the best karaoke singer in the world is, the mirror tells her it is Snow White. The stepmother decides to get rid of her.

4. Make a movie poster. Follow the example.

5. When you finish, hold a movie press conference.

a. One member of the group interviews the actors. Use the questions from Lesson 5.

b. Other members of the group are the actors answering questions about the new movie.

9 *Friendship*

Qualities of a friend

Brainstorming

1. What qualities define a friend? Complete the sentences with words from the box.

☐ *dependable* ☐ *generous* ☑ *kind*
☐ *funny* ☐ *honest* ☐ *loyal*

a. A friend who is caring and helpful is _____*kind*_____ .

b. A friend who makes you laugh is _____ .

c. A friend you rely on is _____ .

d. A friend who tells you the truth is _____ .

e. A friend who is happy to spend time and money to help you is _____ .

f. A friend who always supports you is _____ .

2. Who are your friends? What qualities do they have? Brainstorm and make two lists. Use words from Exercise 1 or your own ideas.

My friends	Their qualities
Lisa	dependable
Josh	friendly, honest

3. Compare your lists with a partner. Can you add more words to your list?

Later in this unit . . .

You will write about a friend.

You will also learn how to write supporting sentences.

1. Read the paragraph and follow the instructions below.

[1] *Lisa is a very good friend of mine.*
[2] *She's dependable and honest.* [3] *She is there whenever I need someone to talk to, and she always tells me the truth.* [4] *She is also very funny.* [5] *If I am sad, Lisa makes me feel better with her jokes.*

Meaning

a. Put a star (★) above the three qualities of a friend that Lisa has.

b. Put a check (✔) above three phrases that give examples of Lisa's qualities.

Noticing and writing

c. Look at sentence 1 in the paragraph. Write a similar sentence with these words.

Bill / my best friend

_____

_____

d. Look at sentence 2 in the paragraph. Write a similar sentence with these words.

Bill / cheerful / generous

_____

_____

2. Compare answers with a partner.

1. Read the sentences in the quiz below. Rank each sentence with stars.

FRIENDSHIP QUIZ

Star rankings

☆ Not important	☆☆ A little important	☆☆☆ Important	☆☆☆☆ Very important

a. Your friend is a good listener: he or she pays attention when you are talking.　　★★★★

b. Your friend is attentive: he or she remembers your birthday and special events in your life.

c. Your friend is secure in your friendship: he or she doesn't get jealous if you see other friends.

d. Your friend is sensitive: he or she always knows when you are upset.

e. Your friend is trustworthy: he or she doesn't tell your secrets to others.

f. Your friend is forgiving: he or she knows that sometimes you make mistakes.

g. Your friend is respectful: he or she treats you politely.

h. Your friend is fun: you can be silly and crazy as well as serious with your friend.

2. Look again at your brainstorming list from Lesson 1. Choose a friend you would like to write about. Write three qualities that your friend has.

My friend's name　　　　　**Three qualities**

Andrew　　　　　　　　　honest, respectful, fun

_____　　_____ , _____ , _____

Supporting sentences

When you describe someone or something, supporting sentences often give examples.

> *Brandon is a good listener.*
> **supporting sentence:** *When I have a problem, he listens carefully.*
> **supporting sentence:** *He always lets me finish what I want to say before he speaks.*

1. Complete the sentences with the names of people you know. Then write supporting sentences.

a. _____ is fun.

Supporting sentence: _____

b. _____ is generous.

Supporting sentence: _____

c. _____ is kind.

Supporting sentence: _____

d. _____ is loyal.

Supporting sentence: _____

2. Now complete the sentences about the friend you chose in Lesson 3. Then write supporting sentences.

_____*Yoo-Kyung*_____ is _____*trustworthy*_____ .

Supporting sentence: *She never tells my secrets to others.*

a. _____ is _____ .

Supporting sentence: _____

b. _____ is _____ .

Supporting sentence: _____

c. _____ is _____ .

Supporting sentence: _____

1. Look at the examples of special things people would like to do for their friends. Choose something special you would like to do for your friend. Write it here.

_____

I want to have a birthday party for my friend.

I want to help my friend find a job.

I want to take my friend to a soccer game.

2. Write notes about the special thing you would like to do for your friend. Follow the example.

My Friend	Naoki
I would like to . . .	take Naoki to a soccer game.
Explanation	Naoki loves soccer. He was a member of the soccer team when he was a high school student, and that is all he talks about. Once he even bought me a T-shirt at a soccer game. Next month there will be an important soccer game in a city nearby. I would like to buy tickets for the game and take him. That would make Naoki very happy!

My Friend	
I would like to . . .	
Explanation	

3. Show your chart to a partner. Is there anything you want to add or change?

1. You are going to write about one of your friends. First, read Jane's paragraphs and follow the instructions below.

Carla from Brazil is one of my best friends. As a friend, Carla is honest, dependable, and trustworthy. She is honest because she always tells me the truth about everything — even about how I look. She is dependable because she always does what she says she is going to do. Finally, Carla is trustworthy because she never tells anyone the secrets I tell her.

Carla is far away from her home now, and the winter holidays are coming. I think it will be a lonely time for her, so I would like to invite her to come and stay at my house with my family. I think she will enjoy learning about our customs and teaching us about hers. I hope the two weeks we spend together will help us stay friends forever, even after she goes back to Brazil.

a. Underline the topic sentence in the first paragraph.

b. Put a star (★) above the three qualities of a friend Carla has.

c. Circle the sentences that give examples of her qualities.

d. Draw a box around the sentence that tells what Jane would like to do for Carla.

2. Now write your paragraphs about your friend.

Remember to write:

Paragraph 1: My friend	Paragraph 2: Something for my friend
✎ a topic sentence	✎ a topic sentence
✎ the qualities of your friend and examples	✎ what you would like to do for your friend

In your journal . . .

Write about what kind of a friend you are. What are your best qualities?

To show a result, combine sentences with so. Use a comma after
the first sentence and before so.

Result

I think it will be a lonely time for Carla.   I would like to invite her to my house.

I think it will be a lonely time for Carla, **so** I would like to invite her to my house.

1. Read the pairs of sentences. Check (✔) the result. Then rewrite them as one
sentence with *so*.

a. ☑ I want to take him to a soccer game.   *Naoki loves soccer, so I want to*
   ☐ Naoki loves soccer.   *take him to a soccer game.*

b. ☐ Laura never tells secrets.   _____
   ☐ I know I can trust her.   _____

c. ☐ She knows a lot about me.   _____
   ☐ I have known Sasha since we were six.   _____

d. ☐ I am lonely.   _____
   ☐ My best friend moved away. _____

e. ☐ Paul is kind.   _____
   ☐ I can always ask him for help.   _____

f. ☐ I will lend him some money.   _____
   ☐ Ryan needs to buy a new soccer ball.   _____

g. ☐ She always makes me laugh.   _____
   ☐ My friend tells great jokes.   _____

h. ☐ My best friend loves video games.   _____
   ☐ I will buy him some new software.   _____

2. Now look at the paragraphs you wrote in Lesson 6. Are there any sentences you
could combine with *so*?

What do you think?

1. Exchange the paragraphs you wrote in Lesson 6 with a partner. Read your partner's paragraphs and follow the instructions below.

a. Read the sentences and check (✔) the appropriate box.

	Yes	No
Your partner wrote a topic sentence for the first paragraph.	☐	☐
Your partner wrote a topic sentence for the second paragraph.	☐	☐

b. Complete the chart about your partner's friend. Use words or phrases, not sentences.

The friend's qualities	Supporting words and phrases
honest	isn't afraid to disagree

c. What would your partner like to do for his or her friend? Write it here.

_____

_____

d. Circle one word to describe your partner's friend. You can write your own word.

fun   interesting   loyal   unusual   warm _____

2. Write a short letter to your partner. Write something you like and a question you have.

Dear Mayuko,

    I really liked hearing about how you met your friend Hee-Young and what she is like. How long have you known her? She sounds like a good friend!

Your friend,

Victor

3. Show your letter to your partner.

1. You are going to write an article about a classmate. First, read the article about Su-Chen.

Su-Chen, Dolphin Lover

Everyone knows that Su-Chen is one of the most friendly, generous, and sensitive students in our class, but did you also know she is fascinated by dolphins? Su-Chen, who comes from Taiwan, loves everything about the ocean, especially the animals that live there. Swimming is her favorite sport, but she likes sailing, too. She likes to read, especially stories about the sea. She says she wants to learn the language of dolphins. Su-Chen dreams about traveling to a special place where she can swim and communicate with dolphins.

SU-CHEN, playing with the dolphins.

2. Interview a classmate. Find some interesting things to write about. Ask about topics like these.

dreams and future plans   *family and friends*   *interests*   *life outside of school*

3. Write three interesting things you've learned about your classmate.

_____ , _____ , _____

4. Write the article. Then show it to your classmate to make sure the information is correct. Make any necessary changes.

5. Write a title for your article.

_____

6. Draw a picture of your classmate or ask your classmate to give you a photo to put in the article.

Unit 10 Superhero powers

Brainstorming

1. Look at Mightyman's superhero powers. What can he do?
Match the words in the box to the pictures.

☑ *become invisible*   ☐ *read minds*   ☐ *speak ten languages*
☐ *fly*   ☐ *see through walls*   ☐ *stop a train*

Mightyman can . . .

become invisible

2. What superhero powers would you like to have? Brainstorm and make a list.

✏ I'd like to . . .

fly
see the future

3. Compare answers with a partner. Can you add more superhero powers to your list?

Later in this unit . . .

You will write about superhero powers.

You will also learn how to write about situations that are not real.

1. Read the paragraph and follow the instructions below.

> [1] *I am often late for work because of traffic jams.* [2] *I wish I could fly.* [3] *If I could fly, I would be able to get to work on time.* [4] *I would fly to my desk on the 12th floor without using the elevator.* [5] *Then I would go into my office through the window.*

Meaning

a. Underline the sentence that explains a problem.

b. Look at sentence 3 in the paragraph. What does it do? Check (✔) the correct answer.

☐ begins a story

☐ describes a place

☐ explains how to solve a problem

Noticing and writing

c. Look at sentence 2 in the paragraph. Write a similar sentence with these words.

wish / see the future

_____

_____

d. Look at sentence 3 in the paragraph. Write a similar sentence with these words.

see the future / invest money in stocks

_____

_____

2. Compare answers with a partner.

Expressing wishes I

1. Write sentences for the superhero powers in the pictures.

a ☑ *fly*

b ☐ *see through walls*

c ☐ *travel through time*

d ☐ *read minds*

e ☐ *become invisible*

f ☐ *breathe underwater*

a. <u>I wish I could fly.</u>

b. _____

c. _____

d. _____

e. _____

f. _____

2. Tell your partner to choose a superhero power from Exercise 1.
Find the power in the chart below and tell your partner what it
might mean. Does your partner agree? Follow the example.

If you wish you could . . .	it might mean you . . .	If you wish you could . . .	it might mean you . . .
fly	■ feel pressure in your life. ■ like adventure.	read minds	■ don't like to talk. ■ are interested in psychology.
see through walls	■ worry about what other people are doing. ■ like watching people.	become invisible	■ are shy. ■ like to go places secretly.
travel through time	■ are bored and want something new. ■ are interested in history.	breathe underwater	■ have a fear of drowning. ■ want to explore the sea.

*If you wish you could fly, it might mean you feel
pressure in your life or you like adventure.*

*Well, I feel pressure, but
I don't like adventure.*

Choosing superhero powers

1. Read Jamie's wishes about superhero powers. Then match the superhero powers with the problems they can solve. You can use each superhero power twice.

1 I wish I could fly.

2 I wish I could talk to animals.

3 I wish I could travel back in time.

a. __2__ I can't communicate with my dog.

b. _____ I want to meet Shakespeare.

c. _____ I don't like to take the train.

d. _____ I don't have enough money to go abroad.

e. _____ I want to tell the birds to be quieter in the morning.

f. _____ I made a terrible mistake when I was a high school student.

2. What superhero powers would you like to have? What problems can they solve? Complete the chart. Follow the example.

I wish I could . . .	The problems they can solve
■ I wish I could talk to animals.	■ I can't communicate with my dog.
■	
■	
■	

3. Interview your partner about his or her powers. Ask questions like these.

■ What superhero powers did you choose?

■ What problems can they solve?

Situations that aren't real

Write about situations that aren't real like this.

I wish I could talk to animals.
If I could talk to animals, I would communicate with Ginger, my dog.

1. Read Jamie's notes. Then write sentences from his notes. Use *could* and *would*.

Things I'd do if I could talk to animals

- *communicate with Ginger, my dog*
- *ask her what kind of food she likes*
- *ask her why she's afraid of the vacuum cleaner*
- *teach her how to use the TV*

a. <u>If I could talk to animals, I would communicate with Ginger, my dog.</u>

b. _____

c. _____

d. _____

2. Choose a superhero power you wrote about in Lesson 4. Write notes about what you could do with this power.

Things I'd do if I could _____

-
-
-
-

3. Now write sentences from your notes. Use *could* and *would*.

a. _____

b. _____

c. _____

d. _____

1. You are going to write about your superhero power. First, read about Jamie's superhero power and follow the instructions below.

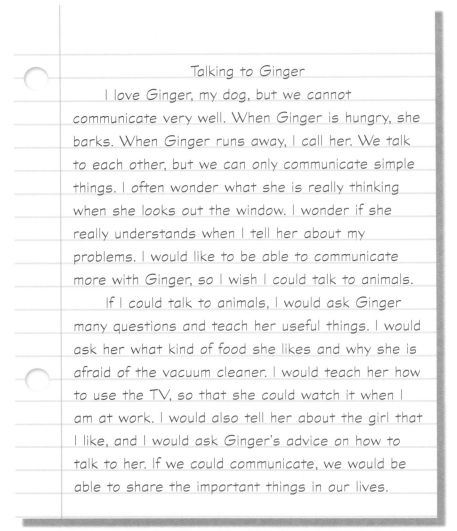

Talking to Ginger

I love Ginger, my dog, but we cannot communicate very well. When Ginger is hungry, she barks. When Ginger runs away, I call her. We talk to each other, but we can only communicate simple things. I often wonder what she is really thinking when she looks out the window. I wonder if she really understands when I tell her about my problems. I would like to be able to communicate more with Ginger, so I wish I could talk to animals.

If I could talk to animals, I would ask Ginger many questions and teach her useful things. I would ask her what kind of food she likes and why she is afraid of the vacuum cleaner. I would teach her how to use the TV, so that she could watch it when I am at work. I would also tell her about the girl that I like, and I would ask Ginger's advice on how to talk to her. If we could communicate, we would be able to share the important things in our lives.

a. Underline the topic sentence in each paragraph.

b. Put a star (★) above the seven things that Jamie would do with the superpower.

c. What does the concluding sentence in each paragraph do? Check (✔) the correct answer.

Paragraph 1	Paragraph 2
☐ It explains a problem.	☐ It finishes the story about Ginger.
☐ It explains a way to solve a problem.	☐ It adds more details.
☐ It shows why Jamie loves Ginger.	☐ It explains why the superhero power would be important to Jamie.

2. Plan your paragraphs about your superhero power.

 a. Write these things for your first paragraph.

Paragraph 1: My problem and the superhero power I would like

✎ a topic sentence (Explain your problem.) _____

_____

✎ additional details about your problem _____

_____

_____

✎ a concluding sentence (the superhero power you would like to have and why)

_____

_____

---

 b. Write these things for your second paragraph.

Paragraph 2: What I would do with the superhero power

✎ a topic sentence (State what you would do with the power.) _____

_____

✎ examples of what you would do _____

_____

_____

✎ a concluding sentence (Explain why the power is important to you.)

_____

_____

---

3. Now write your paragraphs about your superhero power.

In your journal . . .

Write about a superhero that you liked when you were a child. Describe the superhero's powers and what the superhero did with them. Tell what you would do if you could be like that person.

Write about wishes like this.

I want to be able to fly.
I want to go around the world.

I wish I could travel quickly.
I wish I were a bird.

If I were a bird, I could fly.
If I could fly, I would go to New Zealand.

1. Read the wishes on the Wish Tree. Complete the sentences with *want, were, could,* or *would*.

Wish Tree

a I wish that I __could__ sing better. If I could, I __would__ enter a singing contest.

Tim

b I wish I _____ a millionaire.

I _____ to buy a house.

Angie

c I am 80 years old, and I often feel weak. I _____ to be strong. I wish I _____ be as strong as I was when I was 40.

Audrey

d Tomorrow, I will have a university entrance exam. I am afraid that I cannot pass it. If I _____ smart, I _____ pass the test.

Ka-Fai

2. Now look at the paragraphs you wrote in Lesson 6. Have you used the correct words to talk about wishes?

What do you think?

Giving feedback

1. Imagine that you are a member of an awards committee. You are awarding prizes for the most interesting superhero powers. Follow the instructions below.

a. Work in groups of four. Exchange the paragraphs you wrote in Lesson 6 with a classmate in another group. Read your classmate's paragraphs and complete the chart.

Superhero power	What problems it could solve	What the person would do

b. Tell the group about the superhero power you read about. Discuss each superhero power and vote for the best one. Write it here.

Best superhero power: _____

c. Give awards to the other superhero powers. Choose from the awards below or write your own idea.

Most unusual: _____

The funniest: _____

Most practical: _____

_____ : _____
(your own idea)

2. Write a short letter to your classmate. Write something you like, what the wish for the superhero power might mean, and a question you have.

Dear Jamie,
    I like your idea. If you want to talk to animals, it might mean that communication is very important to you. Do you think . . .

3. Show your letter to your classmate.

1. You are going to make a group of superheroes and write a comic book story about them. Follow the instructions.

a. Work with a partner and create a superhero, or a group of superheroes.

Bird Woman can fly.

b. Give each superhero a special power.

Iron Man can stop bullets.

c. Create a criminal character, too. Give the criminal character a superhero power.

Dr. Cruel can become invisible.

2. Think of a story for your characters. Write notes.

Part 1	Introduce Bird Woman and Iron Man.
Part 2	Dr. Cruel kidnaps the Prime Minister and makes a trap for Iron Man.
Part 3	Iron Man gets caught in the trap by a magnet.
Part 4	Bird Woman finds Iron Man and rescues him.

3. Now make a comic book. Include dialogs and narration.

Bird Woman, flying over the factory, sees Iron Man, caught in trap. He is being held by a giant magnet.

Bird Woman flies down to save Iron Man.

Unit 11 Advertisements

Lesson 1 — Products and advertising claims

Brainstorming

1. What advertising claims do these products make? Match the products with the claims.

Advertising claims

a. _3_ Run faster and jump higher!

b. ___ Quench your thirst!

c. ___ Have a beautiful smile!

d. ___ Feel stronger and look younger!

2. What are products and claims you've seen in advertisements? Brainstorm and make two lists.

Products	Advertising claims
sneakers	run faster and jump higher

3. Compare your lists with a partner. Can you add more to your lists?

Later in this unit . . .

You will write an advertisement.

You will also learn how to write advertising language.

1. Read the paragraph and follow the instructions below.

SUPER SONIC SNEAKERS

[1] Imagine shoes that are so comfortable you'll want to sleep in them. [2] Super Sonic Sneakers are the most comfortable and attractive shoes ever made. [3] If you wear these sneakers, you'll run faster and jump higher. [4] Your friends will envy you. [5] Take off your old, uncomfortable shoes and try Super Sonic Sneakers today!

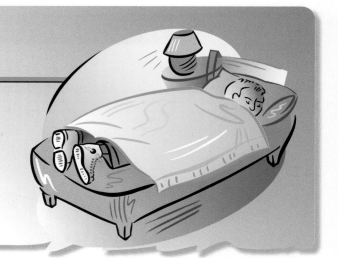

Meaning

a. Put a star (★) above each quality of the Super Sonic Sneakers.

b. Put a check (✔) above the phrases that tell the good things that will happen to you if you buy the product.

Noticing and writing

c. Look at sentence 2 in the paragraph. Write a similar sentence with these words.

Lightning Coffee / strongest / most powerful

_____

_____

d. Look at sentence 3 in the paragraph. Write a similar sentence with these words.

drink this coffee / be able to / study all day and all night

_____

_____

2. Compare answers with a partner.

Learning about organization

An advertising claim tells customers what the product will do.
If you wear these sneakers, you will run faster and jump higher.

An advertising recommendation tells customers what they should do.
Try Super Sonic Sneakers today!

1. Match the sentences to make advertising claims about the products in Lesson 1. Then rewrite the claims below.

a. Wear these sneakers.   _____ You will have a beautiful smile.

b. Drink it when it's hot outside.   _____ You will feel stronger and look younger.

c. Use it every morning and evening after meals.   ___a___ You will run faster and jump higher.

d. Take one every morning at breakfast.   _____ You will quench your thirst.

a. *If you wear these sneakers, you will run faster and jump higher.*

b. _____

c. _____

d. _____

2. Think of a product you would like to advertise. Complete the chart. Then write two advertising claims for your product.

The product	The name of the product
▪ Contact lenses that change your eye color	Eyes for You
▪	
▪	

3. Complete the recommendations with words from the Word File. Then write a recommendation for your product.

a. __Try__ our new Hawaiian pizza!

b. _____ how much better you look with our new hair color products!

c. _____ to our nightclub this weekend!

d. _____ one of these fantastic MP3 players today!

_____

Word File
- ☐ buy
- ☐ come
- ☐ see
- ✔ try

Advertisers use attention getters to get the reader interested in the product.

Attention getters
- *can be a sentence, a question, or just one word.*
- *are often surprising, funny, or make you think about a problem you have.*
- *often appear with a picture.*

1. Match the pictures with the attention getters below.

a. _____ If you like washing clothes, don't read this!

b. _____ No more bad hair days!

c. _____ True love?

d. _____ Heaven is wet.

2. Now write an attention getter for your product from Lesson 3. Then draw a picture in the box.

Attention getter

_____

_____

Writing a testimonial

A testimonial is a statement by someone who uses a product.
Advertisers often use testimonials to help sell their products.

- *"My teeth have never been brighter!"*
- *"Now I get all of the vitamins I need."*

1. Read notes for a testimonial about the Perfect Sleep Pillow. Then complete the chart below with notes for a testimonial about your product.

Before Using the Perfect Sleep Pillow	**After Using the Perfect Sleep Pillow**
■ *had trouble getting to sleep*	■ *now sleep perfectly and peacefully*
■ *had boring dreams*	■ *have wonderful dreams*
■ *woke up many times*	■ *look and feel great in the morning*
■ *looked terrible*	
■ *was tired all the time*	

"I used to have trouble getting to sleep at night. I had boring dreams and woke up many times during the night. I looked terrible in the morning, and I was tired all the time. Then I tried the Perfect Sleep Pillow. Now I sleep perfectly and peacefully, and I have wonderful dreams, too. Best of all, I look and feel great in the morning."

Before using _____ (my product)	*After using* _____ (my product)
■	
■	
■	

2. Imagine you are a customer giving a testimonial about your product. Take turns telling a partner what it was like before and after using the product.

I. You are going to write an advertisement. First, read this advertisement and follow the instructions below.

True Love? Or Just Friends?
Do you ever wonder how that special person in your life really feels about you? Now you can find out!

"I used to spend hours wondering if my girlfriend loved me. In fact, I couldn't concentrate on anything else. But now, thanks to the Love Meter, the answer is right in front of my face! Now I know the truth, and I feel a lot better."

The Love Meter is a tool that measures love quickly, cheaply, and accurately. If you point it at a coworker, friend, or romantic partner, and push the "love test" button, in three seconds you will learn whether that person loves you or not. The Love Meter is so small that it can be hidden in a pocket or bag, so your love interest won't see it. Buy the Love Meter and take it with you on your next date. True love was hard to find before, but not anymore!

a. Look at the advertisement. Circle the attention getter.

b. Look at the paragraph.

- Underline the topic sentence.

- Put a star (★) above the advertising claim.

- Draw a box around the sentence with the recommendation.

2. Plan your advertisement.

  a. Write these things for your testimonial.

The testimonial
✎ an attention getter _____   _____
✎ what it was like before and after using the product _____   _____   _____

  b. Write these things for your paragraph.

My paragraph
✎ an attention getter _____
✎ a topic sentence (the name of the product and what kind of product it is)   _____   _____
✎ what it can do (the advertising claims) _____   _____   _____
✎ a recommendation _____   _____

3. Now write your advertisement. Include a drawing or photo of the customer or product.

In your journal . . .

Write about a product you bought because of an advertisement. What was it? Were you happy with it? Do you think the advertisement told the truth?

Advertisements try to persuade customers that a company's product is the best.

The superlative form of the adjective is often used.

the **newest** model   the **hottest** coffee   the **silliest** movie   the **most exciting** TV show
the **fastest** car   the **biggest** pizza   the **funniest** books   the **most intelligent** pet

1. Complete the sentences with the superlative form of the adjectives in the box.

☐ **big**   ☐ **loud**   ☑ **scary**   ☐ **smooth**
☐ **funny** ☐ **powerful** ☐ **smart**

a. Don't expect to sleep after reading this book because it has some of the

_____*scariest*_____ ghost stories ever written.

b. The Giant Burger Deluxe is the _____ hamburger in Australia!

Just one is enough for your whole family.

c. Get ready to laugh because once again, Lester Jester stars in the

_____ movie of the year.

d. The Awake Alarm Clock is the _____ alarm clock in the world.

You won't oversleep!

e. Beethoven Professional CD Player may not be the _____

CD player you can buy, but it has the _____ sound.

It is good for your ears.

f. Some of the _____ people studying English use

Writing from Within Intro!

2. Now look at the advertisement you wrote in Lesson 6.
Did you use persuasive language? Would you like to add any?

What do you think?

1. Work in groups of three. Exchange the advertisements you wrote in Lesson 6 with members of another group. Read all of the other group's advertisements and follow the instructions below.

   a. Complete the chart below about each group member's product. Use words from the box or write your own words.

creative	fashionable	powerful	unusual	_____
cute	funny	relaxing	useful	_____

	Product name	Words to describe the product
Product 1	_____	_____
Product 2	_____	_____
Product 3	_____	_____

   b. Tell the members of the other group the words you chose for their products.

2. Choose one advertisement to give feedback on.

   a. Check (✔) the appropriate box.

   Does the advertisement include . . . ?

	Yes	No
. . . an attention getter	☐	☐
. . . the name of the product and what it is	☐	☐
. . . some advertising claims about the product	☐	☐
. . . a recommendation and testimonial	☐	☐

   b. Write a short letter to the classmate whose advertisement you chose. Write your comments or questions about the advertisement.

> Dear Meg,
>
>   I liked your advertisement. I thought the testimonial was believable. I would like to buy some Power Coffee! How much does it cost?
>
> Your sleepy classmate,
> Tyler

   c. Show your letter to your classmate.

1. You are going to have a class flea market. Select three or four items that you have with you to sell. Write them below.

_____   _____

_____   _____

2. Write brief advertisements for each item on separate pieces of paper. Be sure to include:

■ *an attention getter*

> **Are sunny days too sunny?**

■ *an advertising claim*

> *If you buy these sunglasses, your eyes will never be bothered by the sun again.*

■ *a recommendation*

> **Wear these glasses when the sun shines.**

3. Display your items. Then look at your classmates' items and ask questions. Follow the example.

A: *I like those sunglasses a lot. How much are they?*

B: *Oh, they're the cheapest sunglasses around! If you wear them, you will protect your eyes forever.*

Unit 12 Lessons learned

Brainstorming

1. Look at actions people sometimes do that they regret. Check (✔) the ones you dislike the most.

☐ *breaking a promise*

☐ *not listening*

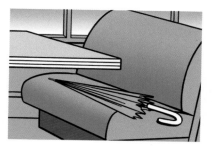

☐ *losing something*

☐ *getting angry*

☐ *being late*

☐ *lying*

2. What actions do you regret? Who did they hurt? Brainstorm and make two lists.

Actions	Who the actions hurt
I got angry.	my sister

3. Compare your lists with a partner. Can you add more things to your lists?

Later in this unit . . .

You will write about an action you regret.

You will also learn to write a concluding paragraph.

1. Read the paragraph and follow the instructions below.

[1] *I will always regret lying to my father.*
[2] *Last week, I forgot that I was supposed to meet my father at the station at 4:00.*
[3] *When I finally got there at 4:45, I told my father that the bus was late.* [4] *He knew it was not true, and he got angry.* [5] *I felt guilty, so I apologized and told him the truth.*

Meaning

a. Sentence 1 is the topic sentence of the paragraph above. Check (✔) another sentence below that could be the topic sentence of the paragraph.

☐ I have problems with being on time.

☐ I've learned that I should tell the truth.

☐ I really like talking to my father.

b. Put a star (★) above two words in the paragraph that describe people's feelings.

Noticing and writing

c. Look at sentence 1 in the paragraph. Write a similar sentence with these words.

feel bad about / stealing / brother's book

_____

d. Look at sentence 5 in the paragraph. Write a similar sentence with these words.

He was angry / said I was sorry / gave it back

_____

2. Compare answers with a partner.

Writing an explanation

To explain an action you regret, write about the situation, what you did wrong, and the consequences of your actions.

the situation: *I told my friend I would go to a movie with her.*
what I did wrong: *I forgot and went to dinner with my family.*
the consequences: *She was hurt. I promised to take her to a movie next week and pay for both of us.*

1. Complete the information below with explanations from the box.

- ☐ My little brother brought his friends into my bedroom to play.
- ☐ She was sad. I said I was sorry, and I'm going to take her to the movies tonight.
- ☐ I promised I would never lie to her again. She forgave me, but I still can't go out for a month!
- ☐ I didn't have enough money, so I could not pay him back.

a

the situation

Yesterday was my sister's birthday. She was hoping I would give her a present.

what I did wrong
the consequences
I forgot to get her a present.
_____
_____

b

the situation

I borrowed $100 from my friend last week. I promised to pay him back today.

what I did wrong
_____
_____

the consequences
I apologized, but he was still mad. When I told him I'd pay him $125 next week, he forgave me.

c

the situation
_____
_____

what I did wrong
the consequences
I got angry and yelled at him.
I apologized for getting angry, and he promised not to do it again. Now we're friends again.

d

the situation
what I did wrong
the consequences
I told my mother I was going to the library to study.
I went to a party instead, and she found out.
_____
_____

Something I regret

1. Look again at your brainstorming list in Lesson 1. Choose an action you regret. Write it here.

_____   _____
             (the action)   (who was hurt)

2. Look at Jenny's notes below about her regret. Then complete the chart below about your regret.

The situation	Last winter, I borrowed my friend Ashley's scarf. It was her favorite scarf.
What I did wrong	I left it on the train.
The consequences	I felt guilty. I couldn't sleep. Ashley was sad, but she forgave me.

The situation	
What I did wrong	
The consequences	

3. Work in groups of three. Take turns telling each other about your regret.

You may write a concluding sentence or paragraph to write about a lesson learned.

Be sure to consider the situation, what you did wrong, and the consequences.

1. Read this explanation. What lesson do you think the girl learned? Check (✔) the best sentence.

I borrowed my sister's CDs without asking.

My sister got angry.

Lesson learned:

☐ I should ask permission before I borrow things.

☐ I shouldn't borrow things from my sister.

☐ My sister is mean.

2. Now read these explanations. Write a lesson learned.

a. It usually takes me twenty minutes to get from my home to my job. Yesterday, I left home exactly twenty minutes before my job started. There was more traffic than usual, so I was fifteen minutes late.

Lesson learned: _____

b. Another student asked if he could copy my homework. I lent him my homework, and the teacher found out. She gave us both a zero on the homework.

Lesson learned: _____

c. I said I was going to school, and my mother trusted me. I met my friend instead. My mother found out, and she stopped trusting me.

Lesson learned: _____

d. At my job, I lost $100. My boss found out. I sent my boss an e-mail saying that I was sorry. My boss said an apology was not enough. I gave him $100.

Lesson learned: _____

3. Think about the action you regretted in Lesson 4. Write one or more lessons you learned from it.

_____

_____

1. You are going to write about something you did that you regret and what you learned. First, read about Jenny's regret and follow the instructions below.

★
Something I will always feel sorry about is losing my friend Ashley's scarf. Ashley had a very beautiful and expensive scarf that she loved. She let me borrow it one day, and I promised to be careful with it. However, when I was going home, I left it on the train. I called the station the next day, but it was gone. I felt very guilty. I told Ashley that I was very sorry. I know that she was sad, but she smiled and said she wasn't angry.

That experience taught me two things. First, I learned that I must be more careful with other people's things. Second, Ashley taught me what true friendship is. She decided that forgiving me to keep our friendship was more important than getting angry at me. I am so lucky to have a friend like her.

a. Underline the two topic sentences.

b. Order the events. Write numbers (1–5) next to the events.

___1___ I borrowed a scarf.

_____ I apologized.

_____ Ashley didn't get angry.

_____ I left it on the train.

_____ I promised to be careful with it.

c. Put a star (★) above four words in the first paragraph that describe feelings. The first one has been done for you.

d. Circle the lessons that Jenny learned.

2. Now write about your regret and what you learned. Remember to write:

/ a paragraph about your regret (the situation, what you did wrong, the consequences)

/ a paragraph about the lesson learned

/ a topic sentence for each paragraph

In your journal . . .

Write about something unpleasant that another person did to you. How did you feel? Did the person apologize? Did you forgive the person?

Varying your vocabulary will help the reader to understand your
exact feelings.

(OK)	When my friend said she liked my dress, I felt **good**.
(more exact)	When my friend said she liked my dress, I felt **flattered**.

(OK)	I felt **bad** because I lied to my father.
(more exact)	I felt **guilty** because I lied to my father.

1. Read the words in the box that describe good and bad feelings. Then write the words in the correct list.

☑ *angry*   ☐ *depressed*   ☐ *embarrassed*   ☐ *proud*
☐ *ashamed*   ☐ *disappointed*   ☑ *excited*   ☐ *relieved*

Good feelings	**Bad feelings**
excited	angry

2. Complete the sentences with an appropriate word from the box in Exercise 1.

a. My friend became ___*excited*___ and dropped my cell phone out of the bus window. I was so ___*angry*___ ! Why was she so careless?

b. I'm so _____ that my friend forgave me. I thought he might stay angry.

c. After Gina said that she didn't want to be friends anymore, I was _____ for a week. I didn't want to leave my house.

d. I thought my friend was an honest person, but I was _____ when she stole my CD. She really let me down, and I cannot trust her anymore.

e. When I forgot part of my speech during the contest, I was so _____ that I could feel my face turning red.

f. After I cheated on the test, I felt so _____ that I told the teacher. I felt _____ after that for being honest.

3. Now look at the paragraphs you wrote in Lesson 6. Do you want to replace any words?

1. Exchange the paragraphs you wrote in Lesson 6 with a partner. Read your partner's paragraphs and follow the instructions below.

a. Write the action that your partner regrets doing.

_____

b. How serious do you think the action was? Check (✔) your answer.

not very serious ☐————☐————☐ *extremely serious*

c. How upset was the other person? Check (✔) your answer.

not very upset ☐————☐————☐ *extremely upset*

d. Answer the questions about your partner's paragraph.
Check (✔) the appropriate box.

Did your partner include . . . ?

	Yes	No
. . . a topic sentence for each paragraph	☐	☐
. . . who your partner upset	☐	☐
. . . when the action happened	☐	☐
. . . what your partner learned	☐	☐

2. Write a short letter to your partner. Write something you like and a question you have.

Dear Eric,
    You did something you regret, but you learned an important lesson. Are you friends with your neighbor again?

Best regards,
Takuma

3. Show your letter to your partner.

1. You are going to make a card with a poem about an action you regret. Follow the instructions.

a. Complete the chart.

Who I will send the card to	What I regret

b. Look at the example. Then write a funny poem about your action. Write the words at the ends of the second and fourth lines so they rhyme like these words.

*I lost your scarf,
And now you're mad.
I'll buy a new one
To make you glad.*

Jenny

bad – glad   wrong – long
forget – regret   blame – shame

_____

_____
(rhyming word)

_____

_____
(rhyming word)

2. Now make the card. Fold a piece of paper twice.

a. Write the poem upside down in the top left box. Sign your name, too.

b. For the cover page, draw a picture and write a phrase like one of these in the lower right box.

- Oops!
- Sorry
- A big mistake!
- Forgive me!
- Silly me!
- I'm sad!

3. When you finish, display your cards on your desks. Later, send your card to the person.

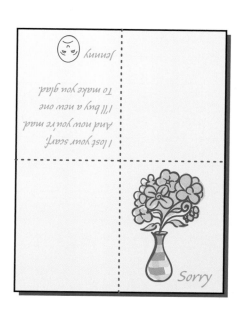